Praise for

THE INVISIBLE GIRLS

"Wonderfully written, the book will have you staring through it, into a world that seems to have been made new. I am grateful there are new writers in the world like Sarah Thebarge. You'll get caught up in the strength of her kindness and the girls she describes even as we gain our focus to slowly see them, and so many others, for ourselves."

—Don Miller, author of *Blue Like Jazz* and *A Million Miles in a Thousand Years*

"Intertwining her own excruciating story of loss and rejection with the stirring story of a family of Somali refugees, THE INVISIBLE GIRLS is a testament to unwavering tenacity, resilient faith, and ineffable grace."

—Karen Spears Zacharias, author of *A Silence of Mockingbirds: The Memoir of a Murder*

"Where is God when it's cancer? If Sarah Thebarge's unforgettable story is any indication, he is closest when the grief is deepest. Don't miss this memoir."

—Katelyn Beaty, managing editor, *Christianity Today* magazine

"Honest, enlightening, heart-touching, and, at just the right times, funny. Sarah's expertly-crafted sentences sing and sometimes sting, flowing smoothly, then suddenly jumping off the page. The interweaving of her story with that of a Somali mother and daughters is masterful. This isn't the American dream. It's a vibrant and authentic story of loss, disenchantment, discovery, and a reawakening of faith and hope."

—Randy Alcorn, author of *Heaven* and *If God Is Good*

"[Sarah Thebarge's] story is a double gift because her raw, honest wrestlings with God free us to be honest with God ourselves, and because her generous passion for the Invisible Girls reveals the healing that comes from pouring our broken selves out for others. Sarah's writing reminds me of Lauren Winner. I loved this wonderful book!"

—Carolyn Custis James, author of *Half the Church*

"I picked up THE INVISIBLE GIRLS and could not put it down. Thebarge fixes a loving eye on a family of Somali girls and an unflinching eye on her harrowing ordeal with breast cancer. No one can lead you out of a desert better than the one who's already been there. Beautiful writer, beautiful book, beautiful soul."

—Susan E. Isaacs, author of *Angry Conversations with God*

"A raw, honest, and powerful witness of the dangerous mercy of God...Her story will humble you and inspire you."

—Rick McKinley, lead pastor of Imago Dei Community in Portland, OR, and author of *A Kingdom Called Desire* and *This Beautiful Mess*

"Very simply: Sarah Thebarge is the best young writer I know, and THE INVISIBLE GIRLS is an incredible story she actually lived out. It's funny and poignant and heartbreaking and it's about people helping each other out. By all means, you should read it."

—Jordan Green, founder of the Burnside Writers Collective and Burnside Books

The Invisible Girls

A MEMOIR

SARAH THEBARGE

MAY 1 2 2014

JERICHO
BOOKS ™

New York   Boston   Nashville

Unless otherwise indicated, Scripture quotations are from the Holy Bible, New International Version®, NIV®. Copyright © 1973, 1978, 1984, 2011 by Biblica, Inc.™ Used by permission of Zondervan. All rights reserved worldwide. www.zondervan.com. The "NIV" and "New International Version" are trademarks registered in the United States Patent and Trademark Office by Biblica, Inc.™

Scripture quotations from *The Message*. Copyright © by Eugene H. Peterson 1993, 1994, 1995, 1996, 2000, 2001, 2002. Used by permission of NavPress Publishing Group.

Scripture quotations marked NLT are taken from the Holy Bible, New Living Translation, copyright © 1996, 2004, 2007 by Tyndale House Foundation. Used by permission of Tyndale House Publishers, Inc., Carol Stream, Illinois 60188. All rights reserved.

Scripture quotations marked KJV are from the King James Version of the Holy Bible.

The author is represented by Daniel Literary Group, Nashville, Tennessee.

Jericho Books
Hachette Book Group
237 Park Avenue
New York, NY 10017
www.jerichobooks.com

Printed in the United States of America

RRD-C

Originally published in hardcover by Hachette Book Group.

First trade edition: April 2014

10 9 8 7 6 5 4 3 2 1

Jericho Books is a division of Hachette Book Group, Inc.
The Jericho Books name and logo are trademarks of Hachette Book Group, Inc.

The publisher is not responsible for websites (or their content) that are not owned by the publisher.

The Library of Congress has cataloged the hardcover edition as follows:

Thebarge, Sarah.
The invisible girls : a memoir / Sarah Thebarge. — 1st ed.
    p. cm.
Summary: "Sarah Thebarge, a female cancer survivor, befriends a family of displaced Somali refugees, battling cultural barriers and sharing their struggle for survival to establish unlikely love and friendship"—Provided by the publisher.
Includes bibliographical references and index.
ISBN 978-1-4555-2391-7 (hardcover : alk. paper) — ISBN 978-1-4555-2390-0 (ebook) 1. Thebarge, Sarah. 2. Christian biography—United States. 3. Refugees—Somalia. 4. United States—Ethnic relations. I. Title.
BR1725.T453A3 2013
277.3'083092—dc23

                                          2012033737

ISBN 978-1-4555-2392-4 (pbk.)

For the Invisible Girls.
All of them.

I am invisible, understand, simply
because people refuse to see me.
—RALPH ELLISON

CHAPTER ONE

ONE YEAR AGO, I was riding the train from the Portland suburbs toward downtown on a sunny fall afternoon when a pair of sparkling brown eyes peeked around the corner of my book, and then quickly disappeared. A minute later, the eyes appeared for a second, and then disappeared again, and I realized the little girl sitting across the aisle was playing peekaboo with me.

I lowered my book a few inches and winked at her. She tried to wink back, but she was preschool age and didn't have the fine motor skills to copy me, so instead she scrunched up both eyes in a prolonged blink.

As she contorted her face, trying to figure out how to wink, I saw that her small frame was covered with baggy sweatpants and a mismatched knee-length print dress, and she was wearing cracked sneakers with frayed laces. Her silky brown skin and bright eyes stood out against the bedraggled backdrop of her clothes, and I found myself captivated by the contrast.

Her mom, who wore a yellow, orange, and red print African dress and a matching headscarf, sat with her head resting on the window, staring blankly at the freeway that paralleled the train tracks. She was short and stout and her skin was wrinkle-free, but her shoulders drooped and her brow was furrowed, making it difficult to guess her age. She could just as well have been twenty-five as forty-five.

A toddler, who wore threadbare pants, an oversized dress, and old sneakers, was standing between the mother's parted knees, trying to sleep while standing up. I watched this child, with her shorn head and chubby cheeks, as she grasped her mother's skirt, trying to stay upright and sleep at the same time. I was thinking, *Someone needs to hold that tired little girl*, when she opened her sleepy eyes and looked up at me. I held out my arms. She climbed into my lap, and less than a minute later she was fast asleep with her head against my chest.

The scene unfolded so quickly, I hadn't had time to ask her mother if it was okay. Now that the toddler was sleeping in my lap, I looked at the mother for permission, hoping she didn't disapprove of a strange woman holding her daughter. Without moving her head from the windowpane, her eyes followed my voice until they rested on my face.

"It's okay?" I asked her.

She looked at her sleeping daughter and flashed a weary smile. "Yah," she said. "No problem."

"Your daughters are precious," I said.

"Yah?" she asked tentatively.

I nodded. "Absolutely."

She smiled again. "T'ank you. T'ank you."

"Where's home for you?" I asked.

She didn't understand, so I tried again. "Where are you from?"

"Somalia," she said.

"Do you have other children?" I asked.

She held up three fingers. "In school," she said.

"Wow, five children! Is there someone at home to help you?"

She shook her head. Her English was limited, so with short phrases and hand motions she explained she and her husband had come from Somalia with their five children, but her husband had left them soon after they arrived.

When she couldn't find the words to tell me more details of her story, she just shook her head, and her shoulders seemed to droop more, bowed low by an invisible weight. "It's too much," she said, repeating her words for emphasis. "It's *too much*." And then she sighed, and resumed her contemplation of the passing scenery in silence.

After a few unsuccessful attempts at winking, the four-year-old gave up her efforts. When she saw her sister was sleeping and her mother was looking away, she climbed down from her seat, walked across the aisle, and wiggled herself up until she was perched next to me on the edge of the narrow seat. She took two dice out of her pocket, placed them in my palm, and closed my fingers around them. She looked up at me, her wide eyes sparkling with anticipation.

"My game," she said. "This my game." Then she tried to pry my fingers away from the dice, laughing, while I pretended my hand was an unyielding claw.

As I played along with the game this little Somali girl had invented, I started to worry about the family. I thought about how overwhelmed I'd be if I were abandoned in a country ten thousand miles from home, left to care for five children by myself with no language training and no money. How would I even begin to navigate a culture that was so different from anything I'd known?

And then I thought about the Golden Rule: "Do unto others as you would have them do unto you." If the situation were reversed and I were a single mom in Somalia and a kind stranger saw me on the train, what would I want her to do? *Help me,* I decided. *I would want her to help me.*

When the mother looked my way again, I took a notepad and pen out of my messenger bag, and asked, "Where do you live?" As soon as the question left my lips, I was relieved I'd had the courage to ask so I could check on them later that week. But I also felt a small twinge of fear that I'd scared this poor woman, who probably already felt vulnerable.

Without saying a word, she pulled a crumpled envelope with a handwritten address from the waistband of her skirt and handed it to me. I copied the address and gave the envelope back to her.

"Thank you," I said.

As we approached the next station, the woman woke up the three-year-old and took her and her sister by the hand. At the next stop, they swept off the train.

As the doors closed, I saw them standing at the corner, waiting to cross the street. The four-year-old was looking back, waving at me. And as the train pulled away from the station, I realized her dice were still tucked snugly in the palm of my hand.

CHAPTER TWO

T WO YEARS BEFORE I met the Somali family, I had escaped from New Haven, Connecticut, to Portland, Oregon. I was fleeing eighteen months of breast cancer treatments that left me physically, financially, and spiritually depleted.

At the end of a grueling course of treatment, which included five surgeries, six months of chemotherapy, and thirty sessions of radiation, I was hospitalized with pneumonia and sepsis. At twenty-eight years old, I lay in a hospital bed for nearly a month, wondering if I was going to live or die. Even the hospital staff didn't hold out much hope for me.

When I went to the ER in sepsis, the resident asked if I wanted to be resuscitated if I coded, implying that because I had cancer, my life might not be worth saving. He even randomly ordered a CAT scan of my brain, saying, "You might have brain metastases we don't know about."

When I had a chest X-ray a few days later, the tech said, "I'm so sorry to have to ask you this because the answer is obvious, but is there any chance you could be pregnant?"

I didn't mind the question, but I was offended by the preface to her question. What was so obvious? Did she think I was automatically infertile because I'd been through chemo? Or even worse, that no man in his right mind would sleep with me because of my disfigured chest? Or that I was already half-dead?

I didn't feel afraid as much as alone. Most of my friends from grad school had moved away from New Haven, my church was defunct, and my family lived a thousand miles away. As the days wore on, I lay there in my bed in the oncology unit of Yale-New Haven Hospital, sinking lower and lower into intolerable boredom and sadness.

Before I had cancer, I assumed that every day a cancer patient was sick, it became easier to deal with the diagnosis. But for me, every day that I was sick, every chemo session I endured, every hospitalization I went through, it became harder and harder because I had less emotional and physical reserve. And I also had less and less support.

During my first hospital stay after my mastectomy the year before, I had more visitors than I knew what to do with. My friends who worked at the hospital came to see me every day. My windowsill, nightstand, and bedside tray were full of flowers and plants and cards.

When I was admitted eighteen months later with pneumonia, even the friends who worked in the hospital didn't come to see me. And I didn't get a single flower or balloon or card. So in addition to feeling sick and tired and feverish and nauseated, I also felt forgotten. And there was no easy cure for that.

My oncologist did his best to cheer me up. One afternoon he sent a yoga instructor to my hospital room. She helped me out of bed and showed me how to do some easy stretching exercises. Then she tried to teach me deep breathing, and I collapsed back onto the bed in tears. "I can't do your deep breathing!" I cried. I pointed to my collarbone. "My entire right lung is filled up to *here* with bacteria."

An art therapist came the next day. She asked me if I'd like to paint something to express how I was feeling. I told her the only thing I wanted was a room of empty walls and a gallon of black paint. She suggested I paint a kitten playing with a ball of yarn. I said no thanks.

A hospital chaplain came to see me after that. She had a hard time making eye contact, and wouldn't sit down in the chair I offered her. Instead, she stood in the doorway, one foot in the room and one foot in the hall, as if ready to bolt at a moment's notice. She asked me what I needed.

Maybe other patients would have been superficial and polite, and just asked for ice chips or a quick prayer, but I was honest with her. I told her I needed someone to tell me how God could allow someone He loved to suffer so much when I wouldn't do this to someone I hated.

She fidgeted and took a step back, until both of her feet were in the hall, and her head was poking through the doorway. She said, "I'll look that up and come back." But I never saw her again.

Before that hospitalization, I had already considered moving to a new town when I finished my cancer treatments. I knew I could never walk down the streets of New Haven, where I'd gone to grad school and worked for the past five years, without having constant flashbacks. How could I function when every street held another scene from the nightmare my life had been for the past year and a half?

After the chaplain left, I knew that moving away wasn't optional anymore; it was imperative. I was beyond the help of anyone here in New Haven. I might even be beyond God's help at this point, but I had to try to live one more time. It seemed my best chance at survival was to start over in a new town. Maybe even a new state. Possibly on a new coast?

I had spent weeks lying in a hospital bed, watching reruns of *Law & Order* and counting the drops of antibiotics, saline, and pain medicine that were dripping into my IV. With nothing but time on my hands, I plotted my escape. I sent a letter of resignation to the clinic where I'd been working as a physician assistant. I sublet my apartment on Craigslist. I sold all my furniture, deciding that whether I died or moved away, I wouldn't need the ratty plaid couch or the watermarked wooden desk anymore.

After nearly a month of IV antibiotics, the pneumonia started resolving and I was discharged from the hospital. I took a cab to my studio apartment a few blocks away. I unlocked the door, dropped my backpack, sank to the edge of my bed, and with my bald head in my hands, I wept.

And then, with tears still streaming down my cheeks, I started packing.

I decided to move to Portland, Oregon, for two reasons. First, it was as far away as I could get from Connecticut without leaving the contiguous United States, and second, I knew the most people there. Well, five. I knew five people there. Five friends I'd made in college in Los Angeles ten years before I got sick.

Some people might have thought about moving back home after a catastrophic life event, but that was a complicated option for me. My father was a pastor who changed churches every few years, and my family moved twelve times before I left for college My parents continued to move after that, so home had always been a moving target.

Less than two weeks after I got out of the hospital, I was standing on the curb outside the baggage claim at Portland International

Airport with two suitcases of clothes. I'd either sold or donated everything else I owned, trying to throw the vestiges of my old life overboard before I drowned in the memories they held.

My face was puffy from taking months of steroids to try to minimize chemo's side effects. My skin was pasty from severe anemia. My hands were bruised and scarred from unsuccessful IV starts and my bald head was covered by an oversized black felt messenger cap specially designed for chemo patients.

I was a broken mess of a girl. As I stood there in the freezing January drizzle, waiting for my best friend, Karina, to pick me up, I gave myself a pep talk. I had started over more times than I could count, and had somehow always managed to be okay. This time would be okay, too. *Maybe,* I thought as the drizzle turned into frigid rain.

Never in my life had I felt so absolutely lost. I had all of my medical records and pathology reports in my suitcase, but no oncologist. I had several interviews lined up, but no job. Karina had offered to let me stay with her and her family until I could get on my feet, but I didn't know where I was going to live after that. I didn't know my way around Portland. And other than five friends from college, I didn't know anyone else in the city.

And as I watched passengers rushing to and from the airport, saying farewell, hugging hello, struggling with heavy suitcases, and hailing taxicabs—I realized that everyone was walking past me as if I weren't even there. As if I were invisible.

CHAPTER THREE

S HORTLY AFTER I arrived in Portland, I had a consultation with an OB/GYN. I had just moved out of Karina's house and into my own one-bedroom apartment. I was home alone when the doctor called me a few days after my appointment and said, "Your test results are back. Your ovaries aren't working anymore, thanks to all that chemo."

"What does that mean?" I asked, suddenly missing my Yale oncologist, who had at least been sympathetic when discussing the possibility that my cancer treatments might cost me my fertility.

"You might as well have a hysterectomy," he said. "You're never going to be able to use those parts anyway."

When I hung up the phone with him, I fell on my bed, pulled the covers over my face, and screamed my frustration into my pillow. Even in Portland I couldn't escape the toll cancer had taken on my body. God was supposed to start giving back what He'd taken, and here He was, taking even more.

And He wasn't just depriving me of fertility; He was taking my identity. I already had a difficult time looking in the mirror and seeing my deformed chest, extensive scars, and bald head staring back at me. I already struggled to feel female, and here He was, taking the last part that made me a girl.

I thought back to geometry class, and to the strict gender roles I'd grown up with. If a girl was equal to the sum of her parts, then a girl with no reproductive parts ceased to be a girl. In that case, what was I? A thing. I was a hideous, malformed, worthless *thing*.

After venting at God for an hour, I began to think that maybe I shouldn't be home alone processing this news. I called Karina and, without going into detail about my conversation with my doctor, asked if I could come over. A few minutes later, I was knocking on her door.

I could hear commotion as she scurried to the door. Her three-year-old and six-month-old were having meltdowns at the same time. She thrust the crying baby into my arms and said, "Could you please take him? I have to go deal with the other one." And she disappeared down the hall.

I walked into the living room and sat down in a rocking chair with the infant in my arms. I began to rock him, and he stopped crying and fell asleep on my reconstructed chest that still felt unfamiliar to me. As I continued to rock him, I nestled my cheek against his sleeping form and thought about the parts I'd never use, and the children I'd never have.

And the tears fell in torrents, mingling silently with his soft blond hair.

CHAPTER FOUR

A FEW DAYS AFTER I met the Somali family, I sat in my car, unsure of whether I should follow through on my crazy plan to show up at their door unannounced. I was worried I'd seem too intrusive, and the family would think they were being stalked by a crazy white woman.

But then I remembered I needed to return the four-year-old's dice to her. I was worried she'd think I had tricked her into giving up her "game" on purpose, rather than understanding I had kept the dice by accident.

So I took a deep breath and started driving. On the way, I stopped at a grocery store and bought a bouquet of daffodils from the floral department, and a clear plastic tub filled with bite-sized coconut macaroons from the bakery.

The address turned out to be an apartment complex in the southeast corner of Portland. The marigold siding on the buildings was faded and cracked, and the warped shingles on the roof were barely visible under a layer of moss and pine needles. I parked on the street and walked toward the complex. Half a dozen children of varying ages and ethnicities were riding bikes in the parking lot. As I approached, they stopped playing and studied me. I waved at them and smiled. *It's okay. I'm safe. You can trust me.* But they didn't wave back. Instead, they watched me carefully as I walked up to the door that corresponded with the address the Somali woman had given me on the train.

I knocked. And then I waited. Dogs next door started barking. I knocked again and heard little feet scampering. The mail slot in the middle of the door opened, and I recognized the shorn head and chubby cheeks of the youngest girl, who had fallen asleep in my lap a few days before. She peeked at me, then dropped the little metal door and ran away, yelling something in Somali.

A minute later, I heard someone unlocking the deadbolts, and the door opened. The woman, who introduced herself as Hadhi, stood there with five little girls.

"Hello, Hadhi," I said. "Do you remember me? I'm Sarah, from the train." She nodded, opened the door farther, and motioned for me to step inside.

From the entryway, I could see the kitchen, dining room, living room, and two small bedrooms that comprised the apartment. The rooms were empty—there was no furniture, and the walls were bare. It was the middle of the afternoon, but all the blinds were drawn and the lights were off, and it was dark inside. I held out the flowers to Hadhi, and she motioned for me to follow her into the kitchen, where she laid them in a few inches of water in the sink.

"Dinner," Hadhi said, pointing to the next room. I turned around and saw that the girls had sat down on the empty dining room floor, forming a circle around a cracked ceramic bowl filled with ketchup. They took turns pulling chunks from a moldy loaf of bread, dipping the morsels in ketchup before eating them. Next to the ketchup was a bowl filled with an orange drink. They took turns passing this around, too, taking long gulps from it before handing it to the next child.

I sat down with them and, with Hadhi's permission, opened the container of macaroons and passed it around. Cookies weren't the healthiest dinner, but they were a step up from moldy bread.

The girls munched on the treats one at a time, studying my face as they ate. I asked them to tell me their names. The nine-year-old, who shared her mom's stocky build, told me her name was Fahari. As soon as she'd said her name, her cheeks blushed with adolescent self-consciousness and she looked away, nervously twisting the edges of her long African dress.

The eight-year-old was thinner and shorter than her older sister, and she had a round scar on her right cheek about the size of a fifty-cent piece. "I'm Abdallah," she said in a soft whisper. As I smiled at her, I wondered how she'd gotten the scar, and what other physical and emotional wounds these girls had sustained in their short lives.

The six-year-old was more engaging than her shy older sisters. When it was her turn to introduce herself, she jumped up, threw her arms around my neck, and hugged me. "I'm Sadaka!" she said. And then she giggled and ran back to her place in the circle.

The four-year-old whose dice I had kept was Lelo. Even in the dim apartment, her wide brown eyes still sparkled. I winked at her, and just like on the train, she contorted her face in an attempt to wink back.

The littlest girl, who'd fallen asleep in my lap on the train, was Chaki. When she smiled at me, I laughed at her mischievous grin and chipmunk cheeks, which were packed with coconut macaroons.

I fished around in my purse, found the dice, and held them out to Lelo. "I forgot to give these back to you on the train," I said. "I'm sorry." She took the dice from my hand as a look of recognition spread across her face and her eyes lit up. She walked over, sat in my lap, and began playing the same game, trying to pry her dice from my locked fingers.

This recognition and familiarity seemed to signal to the other girls that even though I was a stranger to them, I was safe. Their faces and shoulders relaxed. They teased one another, running around, then dropping on the floor next to me. Sadaka asked, "What else do you have in your pok-pok?" as she pointed to my purse.

"I only brought the dice today," I said. "But the next time I come, what if I bring some books?"

She nodded eagerly.

We sat on the floor playing for about twenty minutes, and then I decided I should go. They didn't seem to mind having a stranger in their house, but I didn't want to make them uncomfortable by staying too long.

As I was leaving, Hadhi fished underneath the neckline of her dress and retrieved a silver chain with a heart. She pulled it over her head, and put it around my neck.

Is this a gesture of friendship? I wondered. *Or like a drowning man trying to anchor a rope to a solid mooring, is it an act of desperation?* And then, as Hadhi carefully adjusted the necklace until the heart was centered over my chest, I thought, *Maybe it's not a question of friendship* or *desperation. Maybe it's both.*

She hugged me good-bye, but before she let me go, she whispered, "Come back."

CHAPTER FIVE

W HEN I CAME HOME from the Somali family's apartment that first night, I called my friend Karrie, who was working for an international relief agency.

"Tell me everything you know about Somalia," I said.

In spite of growing up in churches where missionaries to Africa with out-of-date clothes and hour-long slide shows were regular guests, and in spite of attending two Ivy League grad schools that emphasized the importance of being a well-informed global citizen, my knowledge of African geography and culture was embarrassingly scant.

Karrie gave me a brief synopsis of Somalia—a country on the eastern horn of Africa that hadn't had a stable government since 1991. It had been in constant civil war for the last two decades, and the conflict was so violent that its capital, Mogadishu, had been rated the most dangerous city in the world.

Later that night, I lay awake in my bed, unable to sleep. I kept thinking about this family that had gone from instability and violence in Africa to poverty and invisibility in America. What had happened to them in their past? How did they feel about the present? And what lay ahead of them in the future?

The following afternoon I went back to the apartment with a week's worth of groceries, a pot of brown rice, and another pot of chicken and vegetable curry. When I knocked on the door, I could hear them all running from the back bedroom. Lelo and Chaki peeked through the mail slot.

"Sarah! It's Sarah!" they yelled.

A minute later, Hadhi stood in the doorway with all five little girls climbing over each other to see who could hug me first. I made my way into the kitchen and set the food down on the counter. "Do you want dinner?" I asked Hadhi as I pointed to the pots. She nodded.

I looked through the kitchen cabinets for plates, cups, and silverware, but the cupboards were mostly empty. In a box under the sink I found four plates, three forks, and one cup. The only food I found was a bag of moldy dinner rolls. In the fridge there was orange juice, a half gallon of milk, and ketchup.

Because of the limited place settings, we had to eat in shifts. I spooned some rice and curry onto the four plates and sat the youngest girls down in a circle in the empty dining room. I motioned that they could share the forks, but as it turned out, utensils were unnecessary. They all began using their cupped right hands to scoop up food and lift it to their mouths. They did this furiously, shoveling in the food while curry sauce and rice fell on their laps and the floor around them. I didn't know if they were eating with such abandon because table manners weren't part of their culture, or because they were that hungry.

Chaki cleaned her plate in minutes, and held it out to me. "More?" she asked. The littlest girls had two servings each before they surrendered their plates. I stacked the dishes and carried them to the kitchen sink to wash them—only to discover they had no detergent and no dishrags. There wasn't even a bar of soap. So I ran hot water over the plates and wiped them clean with my hand before dishing out more curry and rice for Hadhi, Fahari, and me.

When everyone had eaten, Fahari helped me rinse the dishes in the kitchen sink. "Do you know pasta?" she asked timidly as she stacked the clean plates.

"Of course," I said. "Pasta's delicious. Have you ever tried it?"

She shook her head.

"Would you like to?"

She nodded. "The kids at school say pasta is good."

"Okay, next time I come, we'll make pasta," I promised.

When I'd finished washing the dishes, the girls gave me a tour of their house. As they were introducing me to their life, I took a mental inventory of everything they didn't have. They had no changes of clothes and no pajamas. They didn't have toothbrushes, toilet paper, or soap.

There were two mattresses stacked in the corner of the bedroom that they laid side by side on the floor every night, and they had one gray wool blanket to share among the six of them. Their prized possession was a small TV/VCR unit in the far corner of the bedroom that still had a Goodwill price sticker on it.

I tried to smile while they showed me their house, but my heart was breaking.

After the tour, I packed up my pots and said good-bye. As I was hugging Hadhi, Lelo grabbed my leg and wouldn't let go. I put my hand on her head, and she lifted her bright eyes to look at me.

"Next time you come, can you bring us more food?" she asked.

As I drove home that night, I thought about how vulnerable they were. Unlike most kids, what stood between these girls and starvation was not a mother or a father or a neighborhood or a village, but a stranger they happened to meet on the train.

And I thought about how fortunate I was—that what gave me hope in the midst of my pain and loss was not another antidepressant or another hour in my therapist's office, but the smiles and giggles and hugs of five precious little girls.

CHAPTER SIX

MY DAD WAS RAISED in a Catholic New England family. When he turned eighteen, he declared his intent to enter the priesthood, and his parents were elated. The fall after his high school graduation, they bought him a bus ticket, and he traveled from rural Maine to Baltimore to begin seminary.

But my grandparents' dreams were short-lived. My dad had a front row seat to the scandals in the church that wouldn't be public knowledge for a few more decades. It shook his faith, and he dropped out of seminary after three semesters.

He was stranded in a big city hundreds of miles from home, which for his generation and his budget might as well have been halfway around the world. He took the only job he could find, managing a Pizza Hut.

My mom, Denise, was raised in a Lutheran family just outside of Baltimore. She was hired straight out of high school to be an assistant manager at Pizza Hut, and it fell to my dad, Len, to train her. They fell in love over the dough machine, and at the end of her first shift, as they were balancing the register, my dad asked her out. They were married a few months later, and the following year my older brother, Lenny, was born.

Dad was still interested in going into the ministry, but he found that Protestantism resonated with him more than Catholicism. He enrolled in a Bible college in Pennsylvania, where my other siblings and I were born. Dad finished his theological training when I was three, and took his first position at a church when I was four.

Most children are fascinated with their parents' profession, and we were no exception. When my brothers and I wanted to amuse ourselves, we didn't play cowboys and Indians or cops and robbers; we played sinners and saints.

Lenny was always the pastor, I was always the soloist, and our younger brother Matthew was our first convert. We added my youngest brother and sister to the congregation when they arrived a few years later.

We'd set up chairs facing the piano in the living room. I'd wear Mom's shoes and borrow one of her purses, and Lenny would sport Dad's shoes and a poorly knotted tie. He would stand on the piano bench and deliver a fiery sermon. When he was all out of thunder, he'd jump down and take a seat at the piano. "Now, won't you come, Sister Sarah, and sing the special music?"

He'd wink at me, and I'd trip up to the piano in my high heels and belt out all the verses of "Jesus Loves Me" at the top of my lungs.

When I'd finished, Lenny would say, "Thank you, Sister Sarah, for that blessing."

I'd nod a solemn acknowledgment and trip back to my seat. Then Lenny would strike slow, minor chords on the piano, and in an earnest voice, he'd begin the altar call. While keeping his hands on the keys, he'd turn his head over his shoulder and wail, "Sinners, won't you come to Jesus? Won't you please come?"

This was my cue to round up my little brother Matthew, who was usually roaming about the living room in his walker. Some days he was Arminian, responding to the altar call of his own accord. Other times, he was stubbornly Calvinistic, and it took a strong working of the Holy Spirit (me, minus my heels) to get him to the altar.

Once Matthew arrived, Lenny would lead him in a convincing Sinner's Prayer. And then, while all the angels in heaven were rejoicing, Mom would call us for lunch, which was usually peanut butter and jelly sandwiches served with lemonade. We preferred to call it "Communion."

CHAPTER SEVEN

E VERY SUNDAY WE PILED into the family station wagon and drove to the conservative Baptist church where my dad served as the youth pastor for most of my elementary school years. My parents dropped us off at Sunday school before they went to lead the youth group. Our class always started with songs such as:

My body is a temple, to God it does belong.
He bids me keep it for His use, He wants it pure and strong.
The things that harm my body, I must not use at all.
Tobacco is one harmful thing—and drugs and alcohol.

At this point in the song, we'd jump out of our chairs, hold our fists up in the air, and sing with abandon:

Into my mouth, they shall not go.
When tempted, I will answer, "No!"
And every day I'll watch and pray,
Lord, keep me pure and strong always.

When it was time for the main service, my mom led us down the center aisle in the sanctuary, and we took our seats in a pew near the front. We'd sit in silence as the adult choir, adorned in gold robes with white V-shaped bibs, filed into the choir loft. Then the pastors, including my dad, would walk onto the stage and sit behind the pulpit on two small benches.

After the actors were in place, the organist and pianist would take their respective places on opposite sides of the platform. Fabric screens stretched across the front of the instruments to obstruct any lust-provoking glimpses of the female musicians' calves and ankles.

Rarely, a woman was allowed on the platform to give a testimony or sing a solo. But women were not allowed to read Scripture or lead the congregation in prayer, and they always had to be accompanied to the platform by a man. The man would stand behind the woman until she'd finished speaking or singing, and then escort her down from the stage. This practice didn't strike me as unusual; at the time, it seemed to be the order of the universe. Man was in charge of woman, deciding what she could or couldn't do, dictating what she could or couldn't say, waiting in the wings in case she needed rescuing or, just as likely, rebuking.

My brothers and I usually made it through the opening hymns, the announcements, and the passing of the shiny gold offering plates without incident. But the sermon was nearly always intolerable—a rambling exposition that was more like a yawning infomercial than a compelling narrative.

While my parents were talking to various members of the congregation after church, my siblings and I would go to the church library with the other pastors' kids. In the center of the library was a boardroom table where the deacons held their monthly meetings.

We called ourselves the P.K. (Pastors' Kids) Club. We sat around the board table in overstuffed gold-upholstered chairs on wheels. The oldest kid in our club was Michael, the son of the assistant pastor. He earned our respect because he knew a little bit of Greek.

While our parents were finishing up, we'd sit around the table chatting like miniature, mixed-gender board members—though clearly I was an impostor, since hell would have to freeze over before our church allowed a deacon's chair to be filled by a girl.

CHAPTER EIGHT

W E STAYED AT THE same church until I was twelve, and then my parents decided it was time to look for a new ministry. Many of the churches my dad applied to were small Baptist congregations in rural Pennsylvania and New Jersey. Even though the audiences were small, being the family of the guest preacher made my siblings and me feel like small-scale celebrities. Everyone knew who we were, and sometimes our family bio and picture were even printed in the bulletin.

After my dad finished preaching, our family would walk back down the center aisle while the organist played the closing hymn. When we got to the lobby, my siblings and I would form a receiving line with my parents and shake hands with all the parishioners as they were filing out of the sanctuary. Lots of elderly people pinched our cheeks, patted us on the head, told us they had grandchildren with the same names, and gave us really weird ways of remembering their last names. "My name's Cowperstwait," one elderly man said. "Just remember a cow with a purse on her shoulder waiting in line to get her udders milked, and you'll never forget my name!"

The Sunday afternoon ritual was the same, too. We had to stay and socialize until the last churchgoer's car pulled out of the parking lot. Then the deacons either had us over to one of their homes for lunch or, if their wives balked at cooking for a family of seven, took us to the local diner.

These diners were usually located at truck stops, and the special of the day, which my parents encouraged us to order because they didn't want the churches to think we were taking advantage of their generosity, was nearly always fried liver and onions.

In the privacy of the family car, my brothers and I would debrief on the drive from church to lunch. We would crack jokes about so-and-so's toupee or, worse, the men who spray-painted their bald spots. We complained about the old women who reeked of stale perfume, and the cool kids who excluded us from the Hacky Sack circle because we didn't *really* go to their church.

When we'd finished debriefing about the people, we made fun of the process. While we silently relished feeling important and noticed, we'd complain to my dad that our family was always on display. We told him we felt like part of a politician's family, like we were always trying to make a good impression. My dad might as well have been running for a state senate seat for all the fake smiles we had to muster and all the hands we had to shake.

"Read my lips," my brother Matthew said in a gravelly voice as he held his finger across his upper lip to mimic my dad's mustache. "No new sermons."

My brother Nathan joined in. "Vote for me as your new pastor. I promise new carpet in the sanctuary, hymnals for every pew, and a potluck lunch every third Sunday."

"With no baked beans," I added, recalling that at every potluck we attended there were at least a dozen crock pots filled with the same mushy beans drowning in thick, warm syrup.

"That's right," Nathan said. "There will be a ban on baked beans. And no more Jell-O salad, either."

As we neared the diner, we'd all clap and whistle in approval of the campaign platform we'd created for our dad. And then, as we climbed out of the car, we put on our placid Sunday expressions again. We sat at lunch with our napkins in our laps, ordering the liver and onions special, asking politely for the salt and pepper, never talking with our mouths full.

The deacon who was buying lunch that day would always compliment my parents on how well behaved their children were. And we'd smile and wink at each other—not because we were pleased with the compliment, but because he had no idea that we'd spent most of the twenty-minute car ride from church mocking his toupee.

CHAPTER NINE

T HE NEXT TIME I went to the Somali family's apartment, I took more groceries and some children's books. I knocked on the door, but no one answered. The house was silent. As I sat down on the stoop, listening to the neighbor's dogs barking next door, I was unsure of what to do next. Hadhi had given me the number of her prepaid cell phone, but she understood so little English, phone conversations were impossible.

She had tried to call me one time, and when I answered, she just said all of their names. "Allo, Sarah," she said.

"Yes, it's Sarah," I said. "How are you?"

"Good morning, Sarah," she said, though it was seven o'clock in the evening.

I laughed. "Good morning, Hadhi."

"Yah, Sarah. You know Hadhi, Fahari, Abdallah, Sadaka, Lelo, Chaki…" She just kept repeating their names over and over, as if to remind me of their existence. As if I had another Somali woman who called my cell phone, and I might get them confused.

So as I sat on the stoop, I decided against calling Hadhi. I didn't want to leave the groceries unattended, because I worried someone might take them before they got home. So I sat there and waited.

Half an hour later, the three oldest girls came skipping down the sidewalk with another African woman and her children. Fahari explained that their mom was "at the office," and they'd been escorted home by a neighbor.

I smiled at the mother and motioned that I would stay with the children so she could take her own children home. She nodded and left, and I sat down on the stoop again. The girls opened the grocery bags and shouted for joy at the sight of flour, rice, beans, cheese, and fruit. I took a book from my bag, and read to them while they peeled clementines and ate the juicy wedges.

A few books later, I checked my watch. An hour had passed, and still no sight of Hadhi. The girls asked if I would take them for a ride in my car, but I was hesitant to take children I didn't know very well, and with a significant language barrier, and drive off in my car.

Sadaka told me she had to go to the bathroom. *Great,* I thought. *Now what are we going to do?*

I'd seen a grocery store a few blocks away, so I asked the girls to put on their coats and backpacks. I left the bags of food by their front door, hoping they'd still be there when we got back, and the girls and I walked down to the store. We used the bathroom in the back of the store, and then started for the front door. But getting them out proved difficult. They stood in awe of every aisle, taking in the panoramic view of food.

The girls begged me to buy them food—not sugary cereal or ice cream, but bread and milk and carrots. I explained I'd already bought groceries for them, and there would be plenty of food at their house that week.

When we finally left the store, the girls noticed that in the back of the parking lot, there was a big van with a radio station logo that was broadcasting live from a tent nearby. People were dropping off canned goods and bags of used clothing during a fund-raiser for some local nonprofit organizations.

Sadaka pulled on my hand and said, "Can we take some clothes?"

"No, baby," I said. "Those clothes are for other people."

She kept looking over her shoulder, glancing repeatedly at the mountains of clothes as we walked home.

CHAPTER TEN

M Y PARENTS RAISED my siblings and me with tough love, and they tried their hardest to balance these two elements equally. But I experienced the tough part much more vividly than the love part. I was always more terrified of breaking the rules at the perimeter than I was nurtured by all the love at the center.

Every Saturday morning after breakfast, my parents sent us kids upstairs to clean our rooms. When we thought our rooms were clean enough, my mom came and did what she called "The Inspection." If it wasn't perfect, she'd take the broom and sweep all the toys into the center of the room, and make us do it all again. Sometimes it took five or six hours of cleaning before the room met her expectations.

We weren't allowed to go to movie theaters because, according to my dad, while you might have seen the G-rated movie, someone from church might see you coming out of the theater and assume you'd seen the R-rated movie.

I pointed out that we rented G-rated movies from Blockbuster all the time, and someone could think the same thing watching us come out of the video store. How were they to know that the VHS tape in the little plastic bag was *Chitty Chitty Bang Bang* and not *Hell-*

raiser? It never occurred to any of us that someone who saw you at the movies would actually assume the best of you. Or even more incredibly, wouldn't assume anything at all.

Playing cards weren't allowed in the house because they were used for gambling. And alcohol—well, the evils of that just went without saying. On top of these vices were the strict, gender-specific standards. Menstruating girls were not to use tampons because chastity included not only sexual purity but also an unbroken hymen. Married women were not to work outside the home. Women who wore makeup, or had short hair, or wore pants outside the house were all suspect.

I had to wear dresses or baggy culottes anytime I was at church or school. For most of elementary school and junior high I attended Christian schools, where many other kids came from the same kind of home I did, so I didn't feel out of place. But when I was in high school, we moved again, and I had to go to public school in baggy clothes that were either homemade or bought from the thrift store. Not only was I the new kid, but I was the new kid who wore *culottes*.

There were a few Mennonite girls at my high school who kept jeans in their lockers and changed into pants when they got to school, then back into dresses before they went home that afternoon.

I wasn't that brazen, but I did start keeping chalk and ChapStick in my backpack. When I got to school in the morning, I'd head to the bathroom and use white chalk to cover my acne blemishes (because even concealer counted as "makeup"), pink chalk as blush to color my pale cheeks, and cherry ChapStick to color my lips.

When a Mary Kay lady was invited to our youth group to give the girls a makeup lesson one Saturday morning, my parents wouldn't let me go. Instead, I had to clean the house and then take a five-mile walk to enforce the lesson that spiritual formation was more important than the color of the features on my face.

While the lessons I learned from my parents about concentrating on character rather than looks ended up benefiting me in the long run, at the time their standards seemed unnecessarily severe and added to my perception of God as punishing and implacable.

There are plenty of people who have appreciated the clarity and safety that come from clearly defined boundaries and a view of the world where everything's either black or white. But I didn't thrive. My sensitive soul wilted under the intense scrutiny and untenable pressure.

The expectation of perfection, coupled with the constant fear of failing, made me a very anxious little girl. When I was eight, I started blinking every time our family station wagon drove past a telephone pole. Then I started swallowing three times every time we drove over railroad tracks. I was convinced if I didn't do these rituals the right way, or the right number of times, my family would die. At night I started praying the Lord's Prayer over and over again, certain that if I omitted even one word, God would kill me in my sleep. And after that, I started running the alphabet backward and forward in my head and making patterns out of letters and numbers.

My parents were both one of five children, and our family had five children as well. One afternoon I announced to my parents that our family's birth order (boy, girl, boy, boy, girl) was the same as my dad's if you went forward and the same as my mom's if you went backward. My parents thought I was developing a special gift for math, but in fact, I was developing OCD.

When I was thirteen, I went to the hospital twice in an ambulance because I had panic attacks that made me hyperventilate and sent my heart rate through the roof. After the second episode, when the doctors had determined there was nothing medically wrong with me, a psychiatrist came to see me and told my parents I needed therapy. When I was discharged from the hospital, they took me to see a counselor who was recommended by someone in our church.

The counselor was a Christian man who said he didn't believe in secular psychology. He told my parents there was nothing wrong with me that some Bible verses and a few prayers couldn't fix. They believed him when he told them I was fine, and so they never took me back.

Even though I was just a teenager, it seemed unfair to me that fundamentalism could create severe angst that manifested as OCD and panic disorder, and then proceed to decry the tools created to assuage these tormenting conditions. It wasn't until a few years later that I figured out that the first two letters in fundamentalism are F-U.

At times that feels like an overly critical assessment of an earnest but misguided community, until I remember that I was so afraid of God and all other authority figures that I had panic attacks and wet the bed a few times a week until I left for college.

CHAPTER ELEVEN

H ADHI EVENTUALLY CAME home with the two littlest girls. They had been at the welfare office signing up for WIC and food stamps. She unlocked the door and let us inside, and the girls began to unpack the groceries on the floor.

As they marveled over the bags of groceries in the dining room, I retrieved a box of pasta, some tomatoes and basil and sauce, and went to work cooking them dinner in the kitchen. Lelo asked if she could help me cook. She was too short to see the stove top from where she was standing, so I picked her up and set her on the kitchen counter, and she chattered while I dropped the noodles into a pot of boiling water.

"Do you know Justeen Beaver?" she asked.

"You mean Justin Bieber?" I laughed.

She nodded, and her eyes widened. "You *know* him?"

"I know *of* him," I said, amazed at how quickly this four-year-old had become acquainted with pop culture. "But I don't know him personally."

She gave me a puzzled look. The sentence was too complicated for her to understand. "No." I shook my head. "I don't know him. I'm sorry."

When dinner was ready, I pulled out some plates and forks I'd brought with me. I told them that since we were going to eat American-style pasta, I would show them how to eat like Americans eat. We all sat down in a circle on the floor, and I demonstrated how to use a fork to poke the penne pasta and put it in their mouths. They used their forks for about two minutes, then set them down and went back to shuttling food from their plates to their mouths with their right hands.

After they'd finished eating the pasta, I introduced them to another American treat: ice cream. I scooped chocolate ice cream into cones, and handed them to Hadhi and the girls. Chaki was especially enamored of it. "I like your *fooood*," she said as she skipped around the dining room with her ice-cream cone. "I like your *fooood*."

Lelo finished her dessert quickly, and came to sit in my lap. She put her arms around my neck, and got marinara sauce and chocolate ice cream all over my white shirt. I took a deep breath, trying not to worry about how I was going to get the stains out.

The other girls kept eating their ice cream and, in between licks, asked me lots of questions. *Do you know hot dogs? How do you spell pasta? Did you bring more books in your pok-pok? Do you have a husband? Do you have kids?*

I answered them in turn, finishing with, "No, I don't have a husband. And I don't have kids."

Abdallah began scolding Lelo in her soft voice, motioning that Lelo should get off my lap. Lelo held tighter to me, smearing more sauce on my shirt. "What's the matter?" I asked Abdallah.

"You said you don't like kids, so I told Lelo to get out of your lap."

"No," I said with a smile. "I said I don't *have* kids. But I love kids—I especially love all of you."

Lelo looked up at me. "You love me?" she asked.

I kissed the top of her head. "Yes," I said. "I love you."

She sighed and leaned her head against my chest. I wrapped my arms around her and pulled her closer—closer to the most damaged part of my body, closer to the mastectomy scars that still ached, closer to my heart that, with every giggle and smile and hug from these girls, was becoming a little more trusting, and a little less broken.

CHAPTER TWELVE

WHEN I WAS LELO'S AGE, my stern German grandfather scrutinized my delicate features, and then took my mom aside and told her I was too pretty. He predicted that, if my parents did not raise me with severe modesty, I would grow up to be "a loose woman."

My parents took his words to heart. I wore long dresses and even bonnets sometimes. When I graduated from kindergarten, my parents gave me a children's book called *When I Am a Mommy*. It was a book for little girls that extolled the virtues of getting married, having children, and running a household. My mom wrote an inscription on the front page that said what she and my dad loved most about me were my maternal instincts. Soon afterward, I became my mom's household apprentice. By the time I was nine, I was doing laundry, cooking dinner, and changing my younger siblings' diapers.

My domestic skills were proficient, but I always wondered if there were any other options. I complied with my parents' expectations, but inside I was discontent with the limited options our conservative culture offered girls.

All the women in my family had married before they were twenty years old. None of them had ever gone to college. I read about Florence Nightingale and Jane Austen and Amy Carmichael, women who all had unorthodox but meaningful lives, and I wondered if there was similar potential in me.

When I got to junior high, my mom relayed my grandfather's prediction to me: that I was going to grow up to be a loose woman, that I was too pretty, that my features and my frame were too delicate. I didn't know exactly what sex was, but I was ashamed and afraid of my sexuality already. It must be very bad if my grandfather could see trouble ahead when I was only four.

Instead of wrestling with the realities of appearance and gender, I ignored them. I channeled all of my apprehension into planning a meaningful career. By the time I reached high school, I was reading medical textbooks at bedtime and thinking about college and grad school. I decided if I didn't get into medical school, I was going to go to law school. And after that, I might run for president.

I was going to do something interesting and important, something that didn't have anything to do with being a girl.

I tried to communicate my ideas to my parents, but their vision for my life looked a lot different than mine. When I was fifteen, I was sitting in my bedroom with the window open when I overheard my dad and one of the deacons in the backyard, talking about our family.

"Lenny, he's going to be the next Michael Jordan," my dad said. And it was true, my older brother was an excellent basketball player.

"And Sarah, well, she's going to be the next Julia Child," he said.

I had never heard of this woman before. I opened the window wider and leaned my head out.

"Hey, Dad," I said. "Is Julia Child a doctor?" If my brother was going to be a famous athlete, I wanted to have an interesting career, too.

My dad shook his head. "Is she a writer?" I asked.

My dad looked up at me and laughed. "No, honey, she's a cook."

CHAPTER THIRTEEN

MY YOUNGER SISTER, Hannah, was born with multiple congenital heart defects, which the doctors didn't diagnose until she almost died of heart failure when she was three months old.

When she turned blue and stopped breathing while drinking her bottle one morning, my parents drove her to the pediatrician's office. He sent them to a pediatric cardiologist, who told my parents there was a good chance my sister wouldn't survive her condition. He wanted to send her to the children's hospital by ambulance, but my parents declined his recommendation because they wanted to give us the chance to say good-bye.

I was walking down the hallway at school that afternoon when the principal paged my brothers and me to his office. My dad was sitting there with a pained look on his face. "It's Hannah," he said.

He drove us home, and we stood in a circle in the living room while my parents let each of us hold Hannah for what we all thought was going to be the last time. Then they drove her to the hospital and checked her into the neonatal intensive care unit.

The nurses grabbed Hannah from my mom's arms, stripped her naked, and strapped her to a papoose board while they started IVs.

The pediatric cardiothoracic surgeons came to see her, and scheduled open-heart surgery for the following morning—provided she didn't die of heart failure that night.

After Hannah fell asleep that evening, my parents slipped out of the NICU and went to the roof of the hospital to pray. It was mid-November, and the stars were bright in the crisp night sky. While my mom was looking at the stars, she thought about the story of Abraham, the patriarch who God promised would have descendants as numerous as the stars in the sky.

Abraham's barren wife, Sarah, conceived after that, and they had a child named Isaac. God tested Abraham's faith by asking him to sacrifice Isaac, and by faith, Abraham was prepared to do just that when God stepped in and provided a sacrificial ram instead.

As my mom thought about Abraham and the stars, she also thought about the faith it takes for parents to surrender their children to God's will. She knelt on the hospital roof with my dad, and as they wept, they acknowledged that all of their children were gifts from God that had been given to them to shepherd, not to possess or control.

It took three years of surgical procedures and hospitalizations, but Hannah eventually recovered from her heart defects and grew up to be a healthy girl. After she came home from the hospital, we all had a new appreciation for our family. And my parents kept their promise to God to shepherd us without trying to control us.

So when I told my parents I was applying to a college in California, they didn't object. The school not only accepted me, it gave me a significant scholarship to study pre-med. My parents didn't have the money to fly me out to the college preview weekend, so everything I knew about the school was based on the shiny catalog and a five-minute promotional video I got in the mail.

I flew to Los Angeles the day before classes started. It was the first time I'd traveled west of the Mississippi. From the plane I watched the snaking Mississippi River and the gaping Grand Canyon and the expansive Mojave Desert. I alternated between panic and elation at the distance that would stand between me and my family for the next four months.

On the first day of class, I wore the best dress I had. It was a blue and white striped dress with puffed sleeves and fabric that ended just above my ankles. I'd bought it from the bargain bin at the Salvation Army when my mom took me shopping for my college wardrobe. The dress was about four sizes too big, and the waistline hung loosely around my slender hips. I tied a white bow in my nearly waist-length blond hair, and looking like a character who'd just walked off the set of *Little House on the Prairie*, I went to class.

Though we were all attending a conservative Christian college, most of my classmates had grown up in California, and were much more metropolitan than I was. To their credit, they were much kinder to me than they could have been. Instead of ridiculing me, they were fascinated by my upbringing and asked lots of questions.

You're from Lancaster, Pennsylvania? Are you Amish? Have you ever used electric lights? Have you ever ridden in a car?

A few weeks into the semester, I met Karina in the dorm bathroom. She took pity on me, and decided to give me a makeover to help me fit in better. She took scissors and chopped off my long hair, leaving me with a chin-length bob. She drove me to the drugstore, where I spent five dollars on cheap foundation, blush, and lipstick, and then she showed me how to apply makeup. She rummaged through the clothing donation box in the laundry room on our floor and got me new clothes to wear.

When I walked into the dining hall that evening wearing makeup, pants, and a fitted turtleneck that showed the contours of my torso, my friends clapped and whistled in approval of my new look, and I smiled and took a bow. After a lifetime of hiding—or being hidden?—under yards of fabric and lists of rules, I was emerging as myself. And for the first time in my life, I felt free.

CHAPTER FOURTEEN

AFTER I TOLD LELO "I love you," she leaned her head on my chest and fell asleep while the rest of the girls were finishing their ice cream. Past experience had made me wary of saying *I Love You* to people. I learned the hard way that those words complicate most relationships, and leave you open to more rejection and more pain than if you left them unsaid. But saying *I Love You* to these girls wasn't like accidentally spilling a fine wine; it was like pouring water on parched ground. They seemed as starved for attention and affection as they were for food.

Abdallah sat down next to me and leaned her head on my shoulder. I cupped her scarred cheek, and she smiled up at me, and told me they'd decided on my nickname. "We call you *Sahara Sarah*," she said in her soft voice.

"Sahara Sarah," the others repeated, giggling.

Chaki took my hand and interlaced her little fingers with mine. She pointed to her hand and said a word in Somali, then pointed to my hand and said a different word.

Abdallah translated for me. "She's saying she's African and you're American." Chaki kept chattering in Somali.

"What's she saying now?" I asked.

"She's saying, 'You my sister,'" Abdallah said.

I smiled and said, "I love you, Chaki."

"Me, *toooo*!" she said as she continued to play with my fingers.

After Hadhi cleared the plates and swept the floor, Abdallah and Sadaka said they had a song to sing for me. They stood up together and began singing Justin Bieber's song "Baby."

They swayed together as they sang the first verse. When they got to the chorus, Chaki jumped up and started break-dancing on the floor in front of them.

We all clapped when they were finished. They dropped down on the floor next to me, smiling. Lelo opened her sleepy eyes and looked up at me. "You like?" she asked.

"Yes," I said. "I liked it very much."

After the impromptu concert, Chaki walked to the corner of the dining room, dropped her shorts, and pooped on the floor.

I wanted to run and scoop her up and put her on the toilet, and then drop her into the bathtub. But I didn't want to overstep Hadhi's authority, so I watched the family's reaction. They didn't say or do anything. It was as if this were a normal occurrence. As if pooping on the floor was par for the course.

I thought about cleaning it up for hygienic purposes, but then remembered that there was no soap anywhere in the house. I realized I was more likely to get sick from intestinal bacteria than the rest of the family was, so I left it and said nothing.

But I could feel a panic starting to rise in me. I couldn't eat anything else. I couldn't let Chaki climb on me as she usually did—not with her unwashed hands and poop-smeared shorts.

I quickly packed up my dishes, blew the girls kisses, got into my car, and drove away. When I got home I washed my hands over and over and over again. I remembered the stories I heard from missionaries when I was growing up. They described life in Africa as an exciting adventure, and recounted every story with a glowing smile.

Now, as an adult, I wondered if they'd withheld some important details. It seems to me that anytime you encounter another culture, there is bound to be surprise, fascination, disorientation—sometimes even disgust and offense.

At first I felt like I was being uncharitable for fleeing at the sight of poop on the floor. After all, wasn't I supposed to be magnanimous, accepting, understanding? Wasn't I supposed to be like the Madonna in medieval art, smiling gently on her young charge?

As I turned off the tap water and dried my hands, I thought, *Screw it. We're just going to have to slog through the messiness—'cause those kids are not Baby Jesus.* And I already knew from years of paralyzing doubts and crippling mistakes that I sure as hell was not the Virgin Mary.

CHAPTER FIFTEEN

W HEN I LEFT HOME for college, I was no longer obligated to
attend church, but I kept going, partly out of habit and
partly because I was afraid of what God would do to me if I tried to
quit Him. My church in California was similar to the church I'd
grown up in. Women could play instruments in the church orches-
tra, but they couldn't lead it. They could listen to the sermons, but
they couldn't preach them. They could read the Bible in their lap
silently, but they couldn't read it aloud from the pulpit.

The unspoken message was that, as women, we were beautiful and
valuable—as long as we didn't challenge the existing patriarchal system. As long as we didn't open our mouths.

In my freshman year of college, a guest preacher came to our
church and delivered a forty-five minute tirade in which he stated
that Pope John Paul II and Mother Teresa were going to hell because
they were Catholic, and heaven, of course, was exclusively Protes-
tant. I decided that day that no matter how strongly I might disagree
with the strict dogma or gender-specific standards, I would go to
church for the rest of my life. It seemed wise not to cross the kind of
God who would send Mother Teresa to hell.

In spite of its conservative theology, the college I attended was slightly more liberal than the culture I'd grown up in—girls were at least allowed to wear pants and makeup and listen to pop music. But there were still noticeable lines drawn between genders. Women were not allowed to speak at the coed chapel services that were held three times a week, and female students were excluded from the preaching classes offered by the Biblical Studies Department.

I was a pre-med major, and I spent most of my time in the science department, which was equal opportunity. I competed with male classmates in organic chemistry and calculus courses.

I worked hard—not just to make good grades, but also to earn tuition money. I had to pay my own way through college, so I took extra courses every semester to try to graduate early, and I worked as many odd jobs as I could find. I tutored high school students in physics and biology. I worked as an athletic trainer for the college's sports teams. I served food in the cafeteria. And on Saturday afternoons, I worked as an assistant at a bridal shop. I helped women into and out of every size and style of wedding gown there was. And then I helped them pick out their veil and their shoes and their bridesmaids' dresses.

During my college years, a handful of guys on campus tried to date me. At least I think that's what they were doing. They never stated their romantic intentions; they just slipped me notes asking what my favorite Bible verse was, and what I'd read in my daily devotions that week. I never wrote them back. In spite of the fact that my college and church encouraged marriage, and that I spent every weekend steeped in wedding dresses and tiaras at the bridal shop, I was not in a hurry to get married.

At the church I grew up in, married women often repeated the phrase, "Behind every successful man is a good woman," and winked knowingly at each other. But every time I heard that phrase, I wondered if I could someday find a man who wouldn't always expect me to stay behind, but would at least let me walk alongside him.

Instead of openly challenging the system that treated women as second-class citizens, I countered it with quiet defiance. I turned down potential suitors because I didn't want to be a man's silent half; I wanted to figure out how to be my own whole. And instead of fantasizing about picture-perfect engagements like most of the other girls in my dorm, I plotted pranks to play on the guys who lived on campus.

The night before Valentine's Day of my sophomore year of college, I bribed one of my male friends to steal one pair of underwear from each guy's drawer. He delivered dozens of briefs to me in a paper bag, with a Post-it note on each pair indicating the name of their owner.

With the help of a few girls in my dorm, I strung the underwear up in the lobby of the chapel, and made a heart-shaped name tag for each pair. We snuck out of the chapel lobby at midnight, giddy at the thought of a thousand students' surprised expressions when they came to chapel the following morning. We were so excited at the prospect, we couldn't sleep. Instead, five of us climbed over a locked fence and went skinny-dipping in the college pool.

CHAPTER SIXTEEN

AFTER TWO YEARS of taking upper-division science classes and working up to four jobs at a time, I was exhausted. I decided to take a non-science class, just for fun, to give my brain a break. I'd always enjoyed writing, so I signed up for a journalism elective at the beginning of my junior year. And I loved it. At the end of the semester, the professor asked if I'd ever considered becoming a journalist. The thought had never crossed my mind. I had always considered writing a hobby, not an occupation. The following semester I took another writing course from him, and I was hooked. I didn't just want to write; I *had* to.

At the end of that year, I sat in my pre-med adviser's office crying as I explained to him that I was having a crisis. I was determined to have a career in medicine, but now I also wanted to write. And I was worried that if I went to med school, I wouldn't have the time or energy to write. But if I went to grad school for writing, I'd miss my medical calling.

Instead of insisting that I pick one or the other, my adviser shrugged and said, "Why not go to physician assistant school instead of medical school? And then you can go to journalism school, and get both degrees in the time it would've taken to earn your MD."

So that's what I decided to do.

After college, I applied to Yale on a whim. When I was in high school, my brothers had dared me to send my SAT scores to Harvard, but when the time came to submit my scores, I had lost my nerve. When I took the GRE for grad school, I looked at the list of potential schools I could send my scores to. Harvard didn't have a physician assistant program, but Yale did.

So I sent my GRE scores and a copy of my application to Yale. I got an e-mail a few weeks later inviting me to come for an interview, and I almost fell off my chair. I called my parents laughing, and told them I was going to interview at Yale as a joke, so one day I could tell my kids "I went to Yale," even though it was just for a weekend.

My parents had kept their promise to relinquish control of their children to God, and they supported my plan to interview at Yale the same way they'd supported my college choice. Letting me go to California was harder on them than I'd realized, but the distance had been good for me. Being away from home had helped me become independent, and the distance also gave me perspective on the pressure I'd felt growing up.

I realized that a lot of stress I felt as a child came not only from my parents' conservatism, or my own anxiety, but also from the scrutiny of being a pastor's kid. Whether the pressure was real or imagined, it had always felt like everyone was watching my siblings and me, using both our successes and our failures to their personal advantage. If we succeeded in being loving or obedient, it confirmed that the message my dad was "selling" actually worked. And if we failed, it absolved the congregation from their own shortcomings. *Even the preacher's family can't live up to that standard...*

Growing up in a parsonage next to the church, the scrutiny felt oppressive and unfair. But looking back, having to assert myself against other people's expectations and pursue what I valued no matter what anyone in my family or the congregation thought gave me the opportunity to develop my character. College had been a similar experience. Asserting myself as a single woman in a marriage-driven, male-dominated culture helped me tap into a subtle but sure strength.

When I interviewed at Yale, the admissions committee asked me why they should let me into the program. I looked at them unblinking and said, "Because I'm going to change the world. And I'm giving you the chance to say, 'We knew her when.'"

CHAPTER SEVENTEEN

THE DEAN OF THE PA program called me the morning after my interview. "We know you've been invited to interview at other programs," she said. "But we want you to come here."

I was speechless. I'd only been bold at my interview because I thought I had nothing to lose. They weren't going to let a soft-spoken evangelical girl from Pennsylvania into their program anyway, I told myself before the interview, so I might as well go for broke. The admissions committee told us they weren't going to notify accepted students for a few weeks, but here was the dean on the phone the following morning, offering me not only admission to the program, but a generous scholarship as well.

"I…um…thanks…I…I don't know what to say," I stammered.

"Welcome to Yale," she said.

Attending Yale sounded glamorous in theory, but in reality it was grueling. I attended lectures during the day, then studied in my room until at least midnight every night. I lived on a shoestring budget for the two and a half years it took to finish my degree.

Yale had given me a scholarship to help with tuition, but I had to pay for my own living expenses. I walked a mile to and from classes, even in subzero temperatures, so I wouldn't have to pay for parking. When I went out to dinner with classmates at a Japanese restaurant near the medical school, I had rice and green tea while everyone else had bottles of wine and plates of sushi. When doing clinical rotations in the hospital, I lived off the free coffee and graham crackers in the nurses' lounge so I wouldn't have to pay for meals in the cafeteria.

On graduation day, I walked across the stage and accepted my diploma from the dean of the medical school, and then shook hands with the former U.S. Surgeon General who'd given the commencement speech. My parents were in the audience, and all three of us embraced in a teary hug after the ceremony.

As we took pictures in the medical school courtyard later that afternoon, I remembered the anxious girl who had studied medical textbooks by the night-light, who had insisted on going to college even though no other woman in the family had done it. And now I had not only gone to college, I had finished grad school as well. The diploma I held in my hand wasn't just a master's degree—it was a miracle.

CHAPTER EIGHTEEN

AFTER GRADUATION, I took a job working as a clinician at the student health center on Yale's undergraduate campus. The following year, I was accepted at Columbia's School of Journalism. Twice a week, I took the train from New Haven to Manhattan and studied writing with journalists who wrote for *Time*, *Newsweek*, and *The New York Times*. After I finished my journalism degree, I planned to work as a health reporter for a major news magazine. Since I moved to New Haven, I'd attended a small Baptist church close to Yale's campus. Pastor Josh and the elders and their wives became my surrogate parents, because my parents now lived a thousand miles away in Illinois. The other grad students who attended the church became my closest friends.

A month after I graduated from Yale, I met Ian at the Tuesday night Bible study I attended every week. He was an outgoing, tall, blond-haired Brit who owned a small business in town. He was driving out of the parking lot as I was walking toward my car, and he rolled down his window.

"What are you doing this week?" he asked.

"Nothing," I said. I was waiting for my PA license to arrive before I could start practicing medicine.

"Want to do nothing together?" he asked.

"Sure," I said. I took a pen out of my purse and searched for a piece of paper to write my number on, but I didn't have any paper and neither did Ian. So instead, I wrote my name and number on the palm of his hand.

On our first date, we went to Barnes and Noble and drank hot chocolate while we sat on the floor of the Humor section, reading each other knock-knock jokes.

On our second date, we drove up to East Rock, a cliff that overlooks New Haven, and huddled together under a blanket as the sun set in the golden September sky.

On our third date, he took me to his favorite sushi restaurant and taught me how to eat with chopsticks. As we drove home that night, Rod Stewart's "Have I Told You Lately" came on the radio, and Ian reached for my hand. And that's when I knew he was the man I wanted to marry.

Ian was a Christian, but he was more liberal toward women than the men in my past had been. He encouraged me to pursue my career goals. He respected my opinion. He was the kind of man I'd always hoped to find—a man who didn't expect me to hide silently behind him, but let me walk alongside him as a true partner.

His business was thriving, and with his substantial income, he introduced me to a world that I, who'd grown up wearing thrift store clothes and eating baloney sandwiches, never knew existed. We drove to Manhattan for dinner almost every weekend, and he bought me wine and filet mignon and tiramisu. His friends owned a beach house in San Diego, and we flew there every few months and spent long weekends going to beach parties and swimming in the Pacific Ocean. On one of our trips to California, after we'd been dating for two years, Ian rented a red convertible and we drove from San

Diego to Beverly Hills and shopped for an engagement ring at Tiffany on Rodeo Drive.

In one year, when I graduated from Columbia, we were going to get married and move to Southern California, where Ian would run a surf wear business and I would be a medical writer. We were going to have two blond-haired, blue-eyed kids together, and the four of us would spend summer holidays with Ian's family in England, and Thanksgiving and Christmas with my family in the States.

We had such a good plan, I thought later as I remembered the life Ian and I had dreamed about together. *We had such a good plan.*

CHAPTER NINETEEN

After Chaki's poop incident, I hit a wall. It felt like I'd been sleepwalking, but now I was waking up to reality, and rethinking every decision I'd made with the family.

Why did I hold a stranger's child on the train? Why did I get their address? Why did I think it was a good idea to go to their apartment by myself? What was I hoping to accomplish by spending so much time with them? How could I continue to function as a surrogate parent, teacher, social worker, and nutritionist all at the same time and not burn out?

The other questions I had were less about me, and more about them. When their need was so great, how could I begin to help them? How could I engage with them without Americanizing their culture out of them? How could I help them without making them dependent on me?

And the overarching question I asked constantly—what if I'm doing this wrong?

And then I woke up one morning and read the headline: GIRLS KILLED BY ISLAMIC FIRING SQUAD IN SOMALIA. Insurgents had accused two girls, ages fifteen and sixteen, of being spies. While the girls were screaming and crying, the militants rounded up the town and made them watch while they tied the girls to a tree and shot them.

By the time I'd finished reading the story, I was ready to vomit. The horrific details made me physically ill—and to my shame, put my insignificant struggles with the Somali family into perspective.

So what if forging a relationship with them was complicated? So what if I was uncomfortable? Who cared how overwhelming it seemed? What did it matter if I went a little too far—or not far enough—in helping them acclimate to American culture?

The alternative of living in a country where girls were subjected to unspeakable violence was so much worse than any damage my clumsy attempts to help them could do; I suddenly felt as though I had nothing to lose. So I went back.

That night when I got off work, I bought a take-and-bake pizza and some vegetables and dip, and I showed up at their door. Again, the clamoring to the door, the unlocking of the deadbolts, the hugs, and the exclamations.

I made my way to the kitchen and turned on the oven, then slid the pizza inside. The oven, which looked like it hadn't been cleaned in years, filled with smoke as soon as it heated up. And then the deafening sound of the kitchen's smoke detector filled the small apartment. I quickly opened some windows while Fahari took off her head scarf and used it to fan the smoke detector until it stopped beeping. A few minutes later, the oven stopped smoking, and I walked around the house closing the windows again.

Lelo followed me from room to room, pulling on my hand saying, "Seet down. Seet down. I want to seet in your yap." Finally, I sat down on the dining room floor with the girls, and held Lelo in my lap. But I noticed that Hadhi stayed in the kitchen, eyeing the oven with suspicion.

I wondered what she was thinking. Was she upset that I'd brought the girls pizza? I'd tried to balance it out with vegetables so it wasn't too unhealthy. And I'd brought plenty to share, so hopefully she wasn't wondering if there would be enough.

I called to the kitchen, "Hadhi? Is the pizza okay?"

"Yah, Sarah, yah," she said. But she kept staring at the oven, occasionally opening the door to look at the pizza.

After fifteen minutes, I turned the oven off and set the pizza on the counter to let it cool. "It's no burn," Hadhi said. "It's no burn."

"Hey! I'm a better cook than that," I teased her. "I can at least cook pizza without burning it."

"My food always burn," she said.

"How do you cook it?" I asked.

With Fahari translating, Hadhi told me that she'd used their first batch of food stamps to buy flour and sugar and eggs so she could make her family bread and cakes they were used to having in Somalia. But every time she tried to bake them, they burned. I asked her what temperature she'd been setting the oven. That's when she showed me she'd been turning the oven up to broil every time, because she thought that meant "on."

The family was starving because all their food had burned—because Hadhi had never used an electric oven, and she could read neither English nor Somali. They'd been eating moldy bread the first time I came to the apartment because it was the only food Hadhi could find in the Dumpster behind the grocery store.

After I'd cooked the pizza without burning it, I sat on the dining room floor with Hadhi and the girls to eat. While they munched on the warm slices, they told me more about themselves.

I asked Hadhi how old she was, and she flashed five fingers five times, and then held up one index finger.

"Twenty-six?" I asked.

"Yah," she said.

I thought about the difference between our lives. I was thirty-one and single, and I'd been fortunate enough to attend college and two Ivy League grad schools. She was five years younger with five more children and a whole other life in Africa behind her.

"You're twenty-six and you have five children?" I asked incredulously.

She held up five fingers on one hand, and three on the other. "I've had this many childs," she said.

"*Eight* children?" I asked.

She nodded.

"What happened to the other three?" I asked.

"Three boys. They die in Africa."

I got teary at the thought of how much pain this woman had already endured in a relatively short life, and how difficult her life continued to be. "Hadhi, I'm so sorry," I said.

She shrugged and said, "It's Africa." The phrase seemed to suggest that pain and loss and death were inevitable and unavoidable. And even though that attitude contributed to her resilience, the resignation made me sad.

The mood in the room changed quickly when Fahari tried to clear Chaki's plate, which still had a half-eaten piece of pizza on it. Chaki saw her food being taken away, and her temper flared. She jumped up, planted her feet, and thrust her two index fingers in Fahari's face.

"Fuckie you!" Chaki yelled. "Fuckie you!"

I could tell from Hadhi's placid face that she had no idea her three-year-old was very accurately mimicking American swearing. "Chaki, no!" I said, pulling her into my lap.

She struggled to get free of my arms. "We don't say *Fuckie you*, we say *I love you*," I said.

She eventually stopped struggling to get out of my lap, and sat there pouting until Hadhi and Fahari had washed the dinner dishes and laid the mattresses out on the bedroom floor. The girls asked Hadhi if they could watch a movie, and she rummaged through a garbage bag in the closet until she'd retrieved a worn VHS tape of *Cinderella*.

Before the movie started, I tried to open the blinds and turn on the lights because the room was pitch-black, but Hadhi came behind me and quickly closed the blinds and shut off the lights.

"My mommy is afraid of monsters," Fahari explained.

I pondered this statement as I sat in the middle of the floor in a tangle of five little girls' braids and gangly limbs. They giggled and sang Somali lyrics to Disney tunes because they didn't understand the English words.

When the movie ended, the three youngest girls had fallen asleep with their heads in my lap. Abdallah leaned on my shoulder and said, "Can you sing me to sleep?"

I reached my arm around her shoulder and she snuggled closer. In a hushed whisper, I began to sing "Amazing Grace."

CHAPTER TWENTY

I T RAINED MOST of the day on Easter Sunday in 2006, when I was finishing my first semester of journalism school. I was sitting at the dining room table writing on my laptop waiting for my laundry to finish when I felt a sensation on my chest, like a raindrop had fallen from the sky.

I looked up at the ceiling, and saw that there was no leak. I looked down at my cream-colored silk blouse, and saw an expanding circle of red, sticky fluid over my right breast. I hurried into the bathroom, lifted my shirt, and stared at my bare chest in the mirror. I'd taken off my bra an hour before so I could wash it with the rest of my laundry, and now I saw that the blood that had saturated my shirt was coming from my right nipple.

I held on to the sink and tried to breathe. I knew from my medical training that blood coming from a nipple was a symptom of breast cancer. *It can't be,* I told myself. *It's not possible. I'm only twenty-seven. You can't get breast cancer at twenty-seven.*

In my head, I heard the voice of the OB/GYN who delivered the lecture on breast disease to our physician assistant class at Yale Medical School two years before. He said it could be normal for a woman to have clear or milky nipple discharge, but the woman with bloody nipple discharge had cancer until proven otherwise. He went on to describe what it was like to be with one of his patients in her hospice room as she died of breast cancer at age thirty-six.

It's not possible, I thought as I struggled to breathe, to suppress the panic that was welling inside me and threatening to drown my rational mind. *I can't possibly have cancer.* I was panicking. *Just breathe,* I whispered to myself to try to stave off a full-blown panic attack. *Just breathe.*

I started to cry.

I climbed into bed with my laptop and searched for *bloody nipple discharge* on a medical website I'd used frequently in grad school. The differential—the list of diseases that could cause a particular symptom—was small. Blood almost always came from some sort of mass, the article said. Sometimes it was benign and sometimes it was malignant, but it was nearly always a mass that required surgical removal.

Oh my God, I whispered, in half-expletive, half-prayer disbelief. I closed my laptop, turned off the light, and cried myself to sleep.

Ten days later I went to my surgeon's office with Ian to get the mammogram, ultrasound, and biopsy results. I sat on the edge of the exam table, and Ian sat in a chair in the corner.

Dr. Zink came into the room and leaned against the closed door, my chart clutched under her arms, which were crossed over her chest. She was about five-four with a muscular build and short, dark hair. When she spoke, she clipped her words as if enunciation threatened efficiency.

With a concerned look on her face, she said, "Ms. Thebarge, I'm afraid you have cancer." She opened my chart and held up the pathology report that read, *Positive for malignant cells, suggestive of ductal carcinoma.*

I immediately scanned the sheet to look for the name of the patient that this report belonged to. *It can't be mine,* I thought calmly. *They must have put another person's report in my chart by accident. Clearly, this is a mistake.* But there was my name in the upper left corner, next to my birth date and age.

Sarah Thebarge. Age 27. Ductal Carcinoma.

Dr. Zink said I'd need to have some more tests done, and then her staff would schedule me for a bilateral mastectomy in a few weeks. I rolled the word *mastectomy* over in my head. It was such a sterile, clinical word. But I knew from my experience as a medical professional that when surgeons said *mastectomy*, what they really meant was, *We're going to cut off your breasts and close the gaping holes with sutures that will leave you with massive scars.*

I wondered if this was how people felt on 9/11. You wake up one day with two towers, and by nightfall they're demolished, and you're left with empty craters in their stead. And as you survey the damage, you realize you will never be the same. And you will never feel safe again.

Once I'd processed the reality of the mastectomy, I asked Dr. Zink questions about the recovery period. When I asked about work, she advised me to take at least six weeks off. I asked if I could continue the journalism degree I was working on, and she said I could take summer courses if I felt up to it, but it was doubtful. Then I told her I was supposed to be a bridesmaid in my roommate's wedding in a few weeks.

"Oh, you won't be going to that," she said decidedly. "No, I take that back. You could go, but you'll only be able to sit up for about an hour. They'd have to take you in a wheelchair, and everyone will think you've been hit by a truck."

By the end of the appointment, there was only one question I hadn't asked.

"Am I going to die?" I asked, my voice breaking before I got all the words out.

"Honestly?" Dr Zink said, searching my face to see if I wanted false hope or real facts.

I nodded. "Honestly," I said.

"Well, it's too soon to say for certain. Your prognosis will depend on the pathology and how many lymph nodes are involved. But I have to tell you, breast cancer in young women is very aggressive."

"I can't die—I'm only twenty-seven." My statement turned into a sob, and Dr. Zink stopped talking. Ian got up from his chair and sat on the exam table next to me. I fell against his chest, buried my head in his neck, and wept. Dr. Zink closed my chart.

"I'll give you two some time," she said. She left the room, and gently closed the door behind her.

Ian held me as I cried all my tears into the collar of his white shirt. The hardest thing to understand was not that I had cancer, but that God had let it happen. Didn't He only punish people He was angry at? Why would He sentence me to death by cancer when I'd obeyed Him and believed in Him all my life, even when the easiest or most logical thing to do was walk away?

"I've never left you," I prayed to God as Ian held me. "Please don't leave me."

CHAPTER TWENTY-ONE

WHEN I'D RUN out of tears, Ian walked me out of the doctor's office and put me in the passenger seat of his SUV. I was too dazed to reach for my seat belt, so he leaned over and fastened it for me. He dropped me off at my apartment and kissed my cheek before he headed back to work. My roommate, Karen, met me at the door and gave me a long hug. Then I put down my bag and sat at the kitchen table with my chin in my hands. She stood and watched me as she leaned against the kitchen sink. Neither of us could think of anything to say.

Finally she broke the silence. "Do you want a gin and tonic?"

I hesitated. I'd grown up in a teetotaling household and had been so wary of alcohol's evils that I didn't drink any alcohol until I was a twenty-four-year-old grad student—and even then it was only a glass of wine or half of a cocktail every now and then.

As I eyed the half-empty bottles of scotch and vodka and gin on the counter, which were left over from a party we'd thrown a few months before, I thought about Jesus. When He was in agony, dying on the cross, people offered Him a rag soaked in wine to dull the pain, and He drank it.

Karen looked at me and raised her eyebrows. I nodded gratefully, and she filled a second glass with ice. After she made our drinks, she sat down across from me.

"I don't know how to tell my parents," I said, studying the ice cubes and lime wedges in my glass while I twirled them with my straw.

When I was in PA school, we had a social worker give us a lecture on how to give bad news. He said that before you tell people bad news, make sure you ask them for all the information you think you need—phone numbers, names, addresses—because after they hear the bad news, they won't be able to remember. Try to have a friend or family member there with the person so they don't feel alone in their sadness. Have the conversation in a quiet place. Talk slowly, and use concrete words.

I'd had such conversations in my career as a physician assistant. I told adult children that their elderly parent was dying. I told a young woman that she had a brain tumor. I told parents that their twelve-year-old son had a bone tumor.

But all of that experience didn't seem to matter now. The people who were going to be recipients of this bad news weren't unfamiliar patients; they were my parents. There was no professional or emotional distance between us. This was going to hurt, no matter what I said or how I said it.

I took my drink into the living room, sat on the couch, took a deep breath, and called my dad at work. When he answered, I began to speak, *slowly with concrete words.* "I just got back from the surgeon's office. The test results are back. I have breast cancer." Three simple sentences.

My dad let out a long sigh. He was quiet for a while, and then asked, "Are you okay?"

"So far," I answered, still wondering how long this calm would last. "I don't want to tell Mom when she's home by herself. What I was thinking is that you could drive home, and in about twenty minutes, I'll call and you can be there with her when I tell her."

"Okay," he said. "I'm leaving now."

I watched the clouds ambling by in the blue April sky, and took a few more sips of my drink. When twenty minutes had passed, I called home. Mom and Dad were both on the line.

"Mom, it's me," I said. "I just got back from getting my results at the doctor's office. I have breast cancer."

She started crying. "I know, honey," she said through her tears. "I knew something was up when your dad came home from church early."

"I have to get some more tests done to see how extensive it is. They're supposed to call me in a few days to tell me my surgery date."

"Just tell us when," my mom said, "and we'll be on a plane."

"Okay," I said. "I'll call you when I know more."

And that was the end. It was the hardest thing I ever had to tell my parents, but it was also the shortest conversation I'd ever had with them.

After he dropped me off, Ian had called the pastor of our church, who had called a few more people. By the end of the evening, most of the church knew about my diagnosis. Pastor Josh called and asked if he could bring a few people over to my apartment after dinner to pray for me.

"Sure," I said, willing to accept all the support I could get.

After I hung up with my family and Pastor Josh, I sat on the couch staring out the window, numb with shock and exhaustion. Karen silently refilled my drink, then sat down next to me on the couch. I kept staring out the window, feeling empty and lost.

CHAPTER TWENTY-TWO

As I was finishing my second cocktail of the day, the entourage from church arrived. I couldn't believe it was seven o'clock already. I also couldn't believe that I hadn't eaten anything all day, and I wasn't the least bit hungry now.

I got up from my place on the couch to welcome everyone. There was Jay, the assistant pastor; Matt, one of the elders; John and Anita, another elder and his wife; Josh, the senior pastor; and Don, one of the worship leaders. They all sat down in the living room and looked at me expectantly. Anita was crying.

"If you don't mind, could you just tell us…" Jay began.

I nodded. *Slowly with concrete words* echoed in my head again. "Today I found out that I have breast cancer," I said. "Ten days ago I started having blood coming from my right nipple. I went to my OB/GYN, and she sent me to a surgeon. They sent off samples of the discharge last week. Today I had a mammogram and an ultrasound that showed microcalcifications, which are usually only produced by cancer cells. And the cytology came back positive for malignant cells. In two weeks I'm having a bilateral mastectomy. They're going to take both breasts."

Some of them closed their eyes. Some started to cry. But no one spoke. What was there to say? As I watched them in silence, I discovered something else about cancer. So far that day I had discovered that cancer was terrifying and painful. Now I realized that cancer was embarrassing. I was talking about nipples and breasts and discharge with these men, and I felt vulnerable to and violated by this disease that made my hidden parts everyone's primary concern.

Finally John spoke. "We thought we could have a time of prayer, and Scripture reading and maybe some singing, to lift you up before the Father," he said softly. I nodded. He opened his Bible and began reading from Revelation.

> Never again will they hunger; never again will they thirst. The sun will not beat down on them, nor any scorching heat. For the Lamb at the center of the throne will be their shepherd; he will lead them to springs of living water. And God will wipe away every tear from their eyes (Revelation 7:16–17 NIV).

He closed his Bible and closed his eyes, and Don began to sing "Amazing Grace." We all joined him, singing the old hymn a cappella, in four-part harmony.

We sang the third verse:

> *Through many dangers, toils, and snares I have already come,*
> *'Tis grace has brought me safe this far and grace will lead me home.*

My eyes were closed, and as I sang the words, I got an image of all of us gathered on the banks of a wide, swift river. I was in a white robe, lying on my back on a wooden raft with my arms crossed over my chest. This group was surrounding me, and they gently pushed the raft into the river as they continued to sing:

> *When we've been there ten thousand years, bright shining as the sun,*
> *We've no less days to sing His praise than when we first begun.*

I was dying. They were sending me off to Jesus.

I opened my eyes and the vision disappeared, but the thought stayed. As they continued the living room prayer service, I thought, *I'm dying. They are sending me off to Jesus.*

For more than two hours we sang and cried and prayed. Finally, there were no more words or tears left, and everyone stood to leave. They gave me hugs and kissed my cheek and shook my hand and told me to hang on to Jesus.

As I watched them file down the stairs, I didn't cry and I wasn't afraid. But I couldn't tell if it was Jesus or the gin.

CHAPTER TWENTY-THREE

Sometimes the two weeks between my diagnosis and mastectomy seemed like an eternity; on other days it seemed like no time at all. I continued my routine of going to work and attending church and spending time with friends, trying to keep myself as distracted as possible.

But in the quiet spaces, while I was walking to work or making dinner or trying to fall asleep at night, my mind refused to be still. I thought about the surgery, how I would afford to take that much time off work, what my body would look like after the surgery, how to say good-bye to a part of my body I hadn't even really gotten to use yet.

I wanted to be able to remember what my real breasts looked like, so a week after my diagnosis I met three of my close female friends from grad school at one of their apartments for a topless photo shoot. We opened a bottle of Merlot, and sat around the living room talking about the surgery, the possibility of more treatment depending on the pathology and lymph node biopsy results, and how ridiculous it was to even be having this conversation.

After a glass of wine had made its way to my brain and lowered my inhibitions, I took off my shirt and sat on the brick hearth in front of the fireplace in my bra while my friends adjusted the settings on the digital camera.

When they were ready, I took off my bra and sat there topless in my jeans, with my straight blond hair falling across my shoulders, but it was not a sexy scene. My right breast was bruised and swollen to twice the size of the left breast as a result of the mammogram and biopsy I'd had the week before. There were dark shadows under my eyes from sleeping only a few hours a night since the diagnosis. And instead of trying to seduce the camera lens, I glowered at it with a mixture of grief and defiance.

The following evening, I fell asleep on Ian's couch while we were watching a movie. I woke up to find that the movie was over, and the lights were off. Ian covered me with a blanket, sat down next to me on the couch, and kissed my forehead. The kiss woke me up.

I reached up and wrapped my arms around him and pulled him down on the couch next to me. As I nestled my head under his chin, I began to think of how different things would be after the surgery. My chest would look different. It would feel different. It would be scarred forever.

We had decided to wait until we were married to have sex, and the prospect of having sex for the first time in a post-mastectomy body was horrifying to me. I started to quietly cry. Ian brushed my cheek with his thumb. "I can feel those tears, you know," he whispered.

I started to cry harder, harder, harder, until I was shaking with sobs. "Shhh…" Ian whispered as he stroked my hair. "Shhh…"

I kept crying for a long time. Was it ten minutes? An hour? Under the weight of immense sorrow, I lost track of time.

"Are you okay?" he asked quietly. I shook my head as the tears kept flowing. A while later, he asked again. I shook my head again.

He waited a few minutes, and asked a third time, "Are you okay?"

I pulled away from him and propped myself up on one elbow. "How would you feel if someone told you they were going to have to cut off your penis?" I hissed at him in the dark. It wasn't a perfect analogy, but it was the closest one I could think of at the moment.

"I'd be devastated," he said softly.

"Okay, then. Just let me cry."

CHAPTER TWENTY-FOUR

MY PARENTS FLEW to Connecticut the day before my mastectomy. I picked them up at the airport, and then took them to dinner at a nice restaurant. It was literally my last supper before surgery, since I couldn't eat or drink anything that evening in preparation for next day's procedure, so I ordered anything from the menu that sounded good.

After we'd filled ourselves with lobster, steak, salad, mashed potatoes, and cheesecake, the waiter cleared the table. I sat there sipping coffee with my parents, having exhausted all the easy topics of conversation. Now it was time for the difficult part. I cleared my throat and began talking.

"Just so you know…" I started awkwardly, faltering to find the right words. "If something happens to me tomorrow during the surgery…" My mom started crying, so I made eye contact with my dad instead. "My bank statements and investment papers are in the bottom drawer of my desk. My passport, my birth certificate, and the title to my car are in the fireproof metal box in my closet."

My dad nodded calmly.

"And I also wanted to tell you…" I introduced the next topic just as awkwardly. My mom was crying harder. "If something goes wrong and I don't wake up from surgery, make them check an EEG. If I don't have brain waves, I don't want to be kept on life support. Just let me go." I looked deeply into my dad's teary eyes to make sure he understood.

"It's okay to let me go."

That night I was in my bedroom alone, packing my suitcase for the hospital, when I thought of what my dad had told me on the car ride back from the restaurant. He'd called a pastor friend of his back in Lancaster to ask him to pray for me. When the pastor got the message from his secretary that Len Thebarge's daughter had cancer, he said to his secretary, "I'm afraid you got the wrong woman. Surely it's Len's wife, not his daughter, who has breast cancer."

A sudden wave of anger rushed over me as I thought about that statement, and I shoved the open suitcase off of my bed. Underwear, pajamas, and slippers went flying. I sank down to the floor, weeping, and said, "God, you've got the wrong woman! Twenty-seven-year-old women are supposed to pack overnight bags in preparation for delivering a baby, or going on vacation. They aren't supposed to pack for a mastectomy."

When my anger subsided, I curled up in a ball on my bed, turned out the light, and cried. And as I cried, I prayed, *God, you gave cancer to the wrong person. Take it back. Take it back. Take it back.*

When I woke up the following morning, I took a shower. Just before I turned off the water, I squeezed my right breast one more time, to make sure this wasn't a dream, to make sure the diagnosis wasn't a mistake, to make sure God hadn't lifted His heavy hand and healed me overnight.

I pressed down on my breast, and blood spurted out of my nipple, splattering on the wall several feet away. I hadn't been healed. I was diseased, and I had to go through with the surgery. God hadn't given me cancer by accident; He really meant it. He had sentenced me on purpose.

I turned off the water, kissed the tips of the fingers of my right hand, and touched the fingers gently to each breast. I climbed out of the shower and wrapped myself in a towel, and never saw my breasts again.

Ian came over to my apartment that morning. Standing in the middle of my bedroom, I wrapped my arms around his neck and he wrapped his arms around my waist. I laid my head on his chest, and we stood there silently for a few minutes. What was there to say? Finally I whispered, "I have to get going." He nodded, then pulled me tightly against him and kissed my forehead, and then left for work, promising me he'd be in the recovery room when I woke up from surgery.

At noon, an orderly wheeled me into the operating room, and I scooted from the stretcher onto the operating table, and nurses covered me with blankets. In that moment, I remembered a night in February when I was on a surgery rotation as a PA student. At 2 a.m. I'd been paged to the OR to assist in an appendectomy. A young woman in her early twenties had acute appendicitis. She was beautiful, with a tanned, toned body. They brought her to the OR, wrapped her in a blanket, and the nurses chatted and joked with her until the anesthesiologist placed the mask over her face and put her to sleep. As soon as she was asleep, they stripped her naked, shaved her pubic hair, spread her legs, and inserted a catheter into her bladder. Dignity and comfort were only illusions.

I knew as I was lying there what was going to happen to me as soon as they put me to sleep. But there was nothing I could do about it. The anesthesiologist put a clear mask over my nose and mouth and told me to take some deep breaths. I stared at the bright round lights overhead, trying to stay awake as long as possible. I remembered someone telling me a long time ago that the last thing you think about before you go under anesthesia is the first thing that will come to mind when you wake up. I thought about California, and the feeling of the warm breeze on my face and the smell of salt water in the air and the feeling of warm sand under my feet.

And then I went out.

CHAPTER TWENTY-FIVE

A S I SANG VERSE after verse of "Amazing Grace" to the Somali
girls in the dark, I thought about the painful surgical incisions
on my chest that had healed into dulled scars. I thought of everything I'd lost, and of this new ragamuffin family I'd gained. I thought
about the Somali teenagers who'd been killed, the moldy bread
dipped in ketchup, and the girls' exuberant joy in spite of the siblings
they'd lost, and all the other sorrow they must have experienced in
their short time on earth.

I cried silent tears in the dark as I continued to sing:

Through many dangers, toils, and snares I have already come,
'Tis grace has brought me safe thus far and grace will lead me
home.

After the younger girls had all fallen asleep, I picked them up one
at a time and laid them side by side on the mattresses, then took the
blanket and stretched it across all of them. I kissed Abdallah's forehead, then Sadaka's, then Lelo's, and finally Chaki's.

I paused for a moment as I watched Chaki sleeping, thinking

what a contrast her serene face was to the little break-dancing fire-cracker I'd observed earlier. She was a handful, but my heart over-flowed with affection and compassion for her.

She reminded me of a Bible story I'd been told when I was not much older than her. Matthew 19:14 describes the time that the disciples were trying to keep children away from Jesus. Jesus scolded the disciples and told them, "Suffer the little children, and forbid them not, to come unto me: for of such is the kingdom of heaven" (KJV).

I imagined how out of place Chaki would look in a crowd of well-behaved, well-dressed white children like me and my Sunday school classmates. I imagined how hard she would try to get to Jesus. He would see this little spitfire and say to His disciples, "Suffer that little child to come unto me."

And the disciples would say, "Master, she's the one making *us* suffer. She pulls our beards, smacks us in the face, and takes our food. And she swears like a little sailor. You want even this one?"

As I tucked a corner of the blanket around Chaki's shoulders and brushed my thumb against her full, flushed cheeks, I imagined Jesus saying, "Not *even*. Especially."

I smiled at the thought as I tiptoed out of the room, then sat on the floor in the hallway with Fahari and helped her finish reading one of the children's books I'd brought. Hadhi came from the kitchen with a tray that held a bowl filled with a steaming black liquid, and several legal-size envelopes.

"Somali coffee," she said, gesturing for me to take a sip from the bowl. It was strong, sweet black coffee with a hint of cloves. She told me, through Fahari, that the best thing about Somali coffee is that it fills you up, so even if you can't find food to eat for a few days, you don't feel hungry.

Then she handed me the stack of envelopes—her unopened

mail—and asked me to read the letters to her. I opened the first batch of letters, which was from the public school her daughters attended. The letters said the girls had been tested in English speaking, reading, and comprehension, and had all scored at the lowest level. Because of this, the school was initiating intensive English as a Second Language lessons for them.

"It's bad?" Hadhi asked me, scowling at Fahari. "They bad at school?"

"They're trying really hard," I said, trying to communicate that the girls hadn't done anything wrong. "You should be proud of them for how hard they're trying to learn English."

Her face softened into a smile. "They do good?" she asked.

"Yes, they're doing very good," I said.

The next letter was from the Department of Human Services, explaining their WIC benefits. There was also a brochure listing the foods that were covered by the WIC vouchers. I made a mental note to study it later so I could bring them whatever food wasn't covered by the program.

The last letter was from the Department of Justice. When I saw the official seal in the top left corner, my heart skipped a beat. Were they here illegally? Was it an extradition notice? Had Hadhi done something wrong?

I opened it and scanned it silently. It listed the girls' names, and the name of their father. It said the Department of Justice had investigated Hadhi's petition for child support, but had determined that notifying the father of their whereabouts would put Hadhi and the girls at risk, so they had decided to close the case rather than reveal the family's location.

I had been wondering how to ask her the personal details of their story; how they'd come to the United States and what had happened to her husband and who was paying the rent for their apartment. Until now I'd kept those questions to myself because I was worried if I asked those details too soon, I might intimidate or offend her.

But asking me to open her mail seemed to be a good sign that she trusted me with the most personal details of her life. I hesitated for a moment, because I realized that Fahari would have to translate for us, and some of the details of the story were too ugly for a nine-year-old to be aware of. But then I realized, she wasn't just translating words for me. She'd lived their story, and nothing I could ask her to translate could be as bad as what they must have gone through already.

Hadhi interrupted my thoughts. "What it is?" she asked.

I began hesitantly, "Fahari, where's your daddy?"

CHAPTER TWENTY-SIX

F AHARI SHRUGGED, and then said something to her mom in Somali. Hadhi glared at me, asking why I wanted to know about him.

I held up the letter. "This letter is about him," I explained. "Do you know where he is?"

Hadhi shook her head. "He no good," she said.

With Fahari translating, Hadhi began to tell me their story. She and her husband had been afraid for their lives and the lives of the girls given the unstable political climate in Somalia, so they had fled to a refugee camp in neighboring Kenya. They stayed there for a year, before an aid organization helped them fly to the United States, where they were allowed to stay as political refugees.

"What's the name of the organization that paid for your plane tickets?" I asked Hadhi.

She and Fahari shrugged and said they didn't know. All they knew was that they'd first landed in Arizona. They stayed there for a few months, but Hadhi's husband couldn't find work, so they'd hired someone with a van to drive them to Portland, Oregon. Her husband found a job doing menial labor while she stayed at home with the children. In Somalia, and once they arrived in the United States, he had physically abused her.

I turned to Fahari. "Did your daddy ever hurt you or your sisters?" She shook her head.

"Only your mom?" I asked.

Fahari nodded, and continued translating the story.

Her dad had kept Hadhi and the girls locked in the house while he was at work during the day. They weren't allowed to go outside, and he gave them no money. When Hadhi pleaded with him for some money to buy the girls food and shoes and blankets, he refused. Even when the little girls were crying for food and unable to fall asleep because they were so hungry, he wouldn't budge.

I had been working in an urban ER since moving to Portland. During that time, I had cared for enough domestic violence victims to know that the problem crossed all economic, racial, religious, and ethnic lines. But even though I was realistic about the problem, it still broke my heart that Hadhi and her girls had suffered for so long in silence and isolation.

What amazed me most was not how much they'd been through, but that Hadhi, who had no education and spoke very limited English, was able to get help. Somehow, she had contacted authorities who stepped in to investigate the situation. When the authorities showed up, her husband left suddenly.

State workers referred Hadhi to a domestic violence center and the local Department of Human Services office. Between the two organizations, she and her children had been relocated to a new apartment. It turned out that the week I met them on the MAX and went to check on them was their first week in the new apartment.

Her rent was paid every month, and she got food stamps as well. But that was it. She had no money to buy other things like clothes, toiletries, or bus passes. She didn't even have quarters to do laundry, which was why the girls' clothes were always so dirty.

Fahari said her mom took her and her sisters to parking lots, where they fanned out looking for spare change. They were collecting it in a baby food jar, which she retrieved from a kitchen cabinet to show me. There were a few dozen pennies and a solitary nickel.

I folded the letter and put it back in the envelope. "Let your mom know that she's not going to get child support from your daddy, because the state thinks it's dangerous for him to know where you are."

Fahari translated this, and Hadhi seemed satisfied. "Yah," she said. "He bad man."

And that's when I understood what Fahari had tried to tell me before when her mom was closing the blinds and turning off the lights. Her mom wasn't afraid of monsters in general.

She was afraid of *a* monster.

CHAPTER TWENTY-SEVEN

IN SPITE OF my pre-anesthesia visualization of Southern California, the first thing that came to mind when I woke up from the bilateral mastectomy was not a picturesque day at the beach. My first thoughts were that the recovery room lights were too bright and my chest hurt like nothing I'd ever felt before. Tears were streaming from my eyes before I'd fully opened them.

The monitor over my head began to beep, and a nurse rushed over and shook my shoulder and started yelling, "Breathe! You have to breathe!" Apparently my oxygen saturation had dropped. If I took anything more than a shallow breath, a searing pain ripped across my chest.

I drifted back to sleep, only to be awakened by the alarm on the monitor sounding again. The nurse came back and shook my shoulder and yelled at me to breathe. Now there were more faces. My parents were standing over me.

It occurred to me then that during the surgery my doctor was going to send off frozen sections of the lymph nodes to determine what stage my cancer was. I tried to sit up. My chest was throbbing. "What were my nodes?" I asked my dad through clenched teeth. My parents and the nurse tried to get me to lie back. "What were my nodes?" I asked, louder.

"They were negative," someone said—I can't remember who. "Your nodes were negative. They think they got it all."

I nodded and lay back, and drifted off again.

I woke early in the morning after my mastectomy to a throbbing chest—I hadn't pushed the pain button for a few hours. The surgical team came through on their rounds, and the resident asked how I was feeling.

"Not good," I said. "I'm in a lot of pain."

"Okay," she said abruptly. She flipped through my chart. "We'll add a muscle relaxant. I'm writing you for ten milligrams of Valium." Ten milligrams sounded like a lot to me, but my brain was too foggy to do the math. If it would help alleviate the pain, I would take it.

Later that morning, the nurse came in with some pills, including the Valium. I took them, then asked my mom to help me up so I could walk to the bathroom and get freshened up. She asked if I was sure I wanted to get up right now, why didn't I just rest. But I insisted. I remembered being a PA student, getting up at 4 a.m. to round on patients. I remembered my stomach turning when I smelled patients' morning breath and pre-shower body odor. It had nauseated me, and the worse a patient smelled, the less time I spent in his or her room. When I found out I was having surgery, I determined to keep up with my hygiene no matter how lousy I felt so my doctors wouldn't try to get away from me or hurry out of my room.

I made my mom walk me across the room to the bathroom, where

I brushed my teeth, washed my face, and applied eye shadow and lip gloss. After only a few minutes on my feet, I felt like I was going to faint or vomit or both. I told my mom I had to go back to bed. When I got to the edge of the bed, my legs gave out and I fell onto the mattress and everything went black.

CHAPTER TWENTY-EIGHT

I WAS TOO DEEP into the blackness to move, but I could hear remnants of distant, muffled voices. I heard my nurse call my name, but I couldn't move my mouth or open my eyes to respond. I heard her call for help, and then I heard commotion in the room.

My brain yelled at my body to wake up, yelled that I might be dying. My body groggily answered back that it was too tired to care. There was more blackness, deeper blackness, I was moving away from the voices. I only wanted to sleep, I couldn't fight this exhaustion. I didn't have the energy to care if I ever woke up.

I felt a burning in my arm, and seconds later the black turned to gray, which turned into the white glare of the overhead lights. A gruff male was shaking me and shouting my name. It occurred to me to try to open my eyes before he shook the life out of me. I blinked, and saw the fifty-something, broad-shouldered male medical assistant who had taken my vitals earlier that morning. He was sitting on the edge of the bed, trying to rouse me, while lots of nurses were watching over his shoulder.

"Welcome back," my nurse said. The resident had prescribed twice the amount of Valium I should have gotten—most people my size got five milligrams, not ten. The high dose of Valium, in combination with all the morphine in my system, had made me go unconscious and almost stop breathing.

The Narcan they gave me to reverse the effects of my medications worked in minutes. I was waking up, and as my brain emerged from the fog, my body emerged from the comfort of sleep to an indescribable pain. Less than twenty-four hours after a bilateral mastectomy, every ounce of pain medicine had been erased from my system, and I was in agony.

I began to shake uncontrollably from the shock of the intense pain. My mom found blankets on a cart in the hallway, which she piled on top of me to stop me from shaking. The nurse locked me out of the pain pump for three hours, but I kept pushing the button every few minutes anyway, praying that God would be merciful and allow a few drops of morphine to escape into my bloodstream to dull the pain.

CHAPTER TWENTY-NINE

IN THE MONTHS to come, I often thought back to that incident the morning after surgery. Every time it came to mind, I wished that I had wandered deeper into that darkness, whatever it was. Unconsciousness—or even death—would have been preferable to the hell that was recovery.

I had decided in the two weeks between my diagnosis and my surgery that the only good that could possibly come of this was that I could write a book for other cancer patients on how to survive the ordeal. I decided this book would sell better if it contained lots of pictures, so I made my best friends take photos of me before surgery, and I made my mom take pictures of me after surgery, even when she didn't want to. Even when it made her cry.

When I looked at those post-op pictures later, I didn't want to write; I wanted to vomit. They reminded me of how much emotional and physical pain I was in. In the photos taken on my last day in the hospital, I am pale and thin with dark circles under my eyes and lots of needle marks in my arms. I look like a heroin addict coming down from a bad trip.

After I was discharged from the hospital, my parents drove me to the store to get groceries and my prescriptions. While my dad parked the car, my mom took me by the elbow and led me into the store. I was too proud to sit in the motorized wheelchair, but too weak to stand on my own. So I leaned on my mom's shoulder as we waited in line at the pharmacy counter. When it was my turn, I handed the pharmacist my prescriptions. She looked concerned and said, "We'll fill these as soon as possible" with such urgency, I had to look around me to see who was so sick, who needed medicines so quickly.

And then I realized she'd been looking at me.

CHAPTER THIRTY

A FEW WEEKS AFTER I met the Somali family, I was getting ready to leave town for a week to visit my parents, who were living in Illinois. The night before I left, I had dinner with Hadhi and the girls, then had Fahari translate that I was going to Chicago for a week. Hadhi's jaw dropped. Lelo started crying.

"They are sad that you are moving to Chicago," Fahari told me.

"No, wait, I'm not *moving* to Chicago!" I said. "I'm just going there for a week." I held up seven fingers. "Seven days, and I'll be back."

While I was home, I went to the fabric store with my mom and sister-in-law, and we got yards of fleece to make Hadhi and the girls double-sided fleece blankets. Everything they owned was community property—they had nothing that belonged to each of them personally. We decided to make each blanket a different color and pattern so each girl could have a blanket that was uniquely hers.

The day after I flew back to Portland, I showed up at their door with a large duffel bag filled with blankets, as well as a bag of toiletries.

I hugged Hadhi and gave her a blanket, then sat the girls down in a circle and distributed the blankets one by one. They shrieked and jumped for joy and put the blankets around their shoulders like capes, and chased one another around the living room.

After a few minutes of celebration, I told them I had more gifts for them. I reached into the bag and pulled out toothbrushes, toothpaste, toilet paper, and bars of soap.

They looked at the pile of toiletries with wonder and suspicion. "Do you want me to show you how these work?" I asked.

The girls all nodded.

I led them to the bathroom, and taught them basic hygiene. I demonstrated to them (over their clothes) how to use toilet paper, then how to wash their hands, how to brush their teeth, and ended by miming how to take a shower with soap.

They were so excited about the bar of soap, they stripped their clothes off, and the five of them jumped into the shower together. Screaming and laughing and splashing, they took turns soaping up and rinsing off. Hadhi sat on the floor in the hallway, laughing with them.

It wasn't until they had climbed out of the shower and were standing in the bathroom wet and shivering that I realized something I'd overlooked before—there were no towels.

I grabbed their new blankets from the living room and used one side to dry them off, then flipped them over and used the other side to wrap them up. But even with the blankets wrapped around them, their teeth were chattering.

Why is it so cold in here? I wondered, realizing that I was still wearing my coat because I was cold, too. "Hadhi, your house is cold," I said, pointing to Chaki and Lelo, whose teeth were chattering.

Hadhi looked at me helplessly, as if to say there was nothing she could do.

I looked around the living room. There was a vent in the wall, but no thermostat or "on" switch. After looking around the apartment for a while, I found the thermostat in the hallway and turned it on. Warm air blew out of the vent in the living room, and the girls began running around the house screaming that I had set their house on fire.

"Everybody relax!" I said, laughing. "It's not a fire; it's heat."

We sat around the vent that was blowing out warm air as though it were a roaring fire. As the girls warmed their frigid fingers and toes against the hot metal grate, I scolded myself. I'd been visiting the family a few times a week for the past month. How could I not have noticed until now that they didn't know how to turn on the heat?

After they were warmed up, I told them it was bedtime. They followed me down the hall from the living room to their bedroom with their blankets wrapped around them, trailing on the floor behind them as if they were little African queens wrapped up in royal robes.

While I put the girls to bed, Hadhi finished washing dishes in the kitchen, and then took a garbage bag full of their dirty laundry and started washing it out in the bathtub, using a bar of soap I'd brought to scrub the stains and stench out of the girls' clothes.

The girls lay down on the mattresses and asked me to read them a story. Chaki climbed into my lap and snuggled up to me while I picked up a Berenstain Bears book from the floor.

"I warm," she said with a sleepy smile.

CHAPTER THIRTY-ONE

MY DAD FLEW BACK to Illinois the day I got home from the hospital. My mom stayed for another week. And then I asked her to go home, because I wanted to try to get my life back to normal, whatever that meant.

When I was in the hospital, the nurses had changed the bandages on my chest. And then, when I first got home, my mom changed them for me. After she left, I had to change the bandages myself, which meant I had to look at my post-mastectomy chest for the first time.

I stood in front of the bathroom mirror, the same mirror I'd stood at the month before, watching blood trickle from my right nipple. I lifted up my camisole, and peeled the dressings off the matching six-inch horizontal incisions that covered the area where my breasts used to be. The flat, nippleless skin and large scars were hideous.

I hated the appearance of my chest so much that I undressed in the dark every night after that. In the shower, I turned my head away when it came time to wash my chest. I couldn't stand to look at myself.

In the months that followed my mastectomy, I sank into a deep depression. I was supposed to resume my journalism studies the month after my surgery, but I was too overwhelmed and too sad to think about taking the train from New Haven to Manhattan twice a week for class. So I applied for a medical leave, worked part-time at an urgent care clinic for Yale students, and spent the rest of the time staring out the window at the sky.

I felt so alone in this post-mastectomy world. My roommate, Karen, had gotten married and kept the apartment we shared, so I'd moved to a small studio apartment the week I got out of the hospital. The people from church who'd prayed and sung with me in my living room the night of my diagnosis were missing in action. After I got home from the hospital, no one called or came over to check on me.

One of the deacons at church told me people were signed up to bring me a meal every night for two weeks after surgery so I wouldn't have to worry about buying groceries or cooking. So every night for two weeks I waited in my apartment. But no one came, or even called to say they weren't coming.

I stopped going to church because I was hurt and angry at how these people I'd trusted had abandoned me. Had God forgotten about me, too?

Ian had been distant since my surgery, and every time I asked him for help, he told me he was working late or out of town. I had to eat somehow, but I wasn't allowed to drive or lift more than ten pounds for six weeks after the surgery. I was out of work and didn't have money to order takeout. So I ended up walking half a mile each way to the grocery store a few times a week to buy food.

Every time I went to pick up an item to put it into the cart, I was paralyzed by the fear that whatever I ate could cause my cancer to come back. Every time I looked at any food, I could remember someone, at some point in the past, saying, "They say that causes cancer…"

The pesticide-soaked produce, the smoked lunch meat, the nonorganic milk, the diet soda, the charbroiled meat, the sugar-free syrup, the artificially flavored fruit juice…I couldn't find a single item to buy without trepidation.

It made me want to rewind the tape of my life and go back to those conversations and news reports and articles and demand to know, "What *kind* of cancer does it cause? Do pesticides and Sweet 'n Low and hormones cause *breast* cancer, or just any kind of cancer? And how do you know?"

Standing in the middle of the grocery store, I began to feel guilty. I felt like some warning I had ignored, some story I had dismissed as a myth, had been the key to avoiding breast cancer. If that was true, I was responsible for my cancer. It was my fault. All my fault.

In the end, I selected food based on its weight. Bananas, juice, and jars of pasta sauce made the bags too heavy. So I settled for bread, pretzels, and powdered soup mixes. Then I balanced the bags on my arms, and walked half a mile home.

CHAPTER THIRTY-TWO

EVEN THOUGH IT had been a few months since my surgery, every morning felt as if I were waking up from a long coma. Even simple tasks felt awkward and unfamiliar. Brushing my teeth—*have I ever done this before?* Writing my name—*whose signature is this?* Driving my car—*where are we going?* Washing my face—*who is that girl?* Typing on my laptop—*why is she so sad?* Answering my cell phone—*and why doesn't she just speak up?*

The only person I could talk to about the depression was Libby, the adjunct professor of the first writing class I took in journalism school. She was a lifelong New Yorker, a self-proclaimed bitch who worked as an investigative reporter for a Long Island newspaper.

When I first met her, I thought of her as my antithesis. She was brash and I was soft-spoken. She had curly black hair, and mine was blond and straight. She prided herself on powerful, succinct writing, and I tried to turn each piece I wrote into an expansive literary masterpiece.

At the beginning of the semester, we had been assigned to write an article about the criminal justice system. I was more interested in the guards' uniforms, the marble floors, and the inscriptions above the doorways than I was in the court proceedings, so that's what I wrote about. Libby graded the assignment, and at the top she scrawled in red ink, "Sarah: This piece meanders like the Nile."

When I called my journalism professor to tell him I'd been diagnosed with cancer and would be out for the last two weeks of the semester, he told me, "You should talk to Libby."

I had never talked to Libby about anything except writing assignments, and I had no reason to talk to her now—she seemed unlikely to sympathize with my plight. "Why Libby?" I asked.

"Libby has cancer," my professor said.

A few days later, Libby called me and asked me to meet her in her office before class. She told me the year before she'd been diagnosed with lung cancer at the age of thirty-seven. She had been in remission for the past few months, and she was getting married the following spring, glad to be done with treatments so she could focus on reporting and the wedding.

She didn't seem sad or afraid; the only emotion I could detect in her was anger. She was as angry at God as she imagined He was at her. "Cancer is one big mind-fuck," she said. "When I got my diagnosis, all I wanted to know was, who did I piss off in heaven?"

Then she sat there glaring in my direction, waiting for me to offer a plausible answer.

But I certainly didn't have any answers; I had exactly the same question. At the very least, it felt like God had forgotten about me. At worst, He was angry at me for something I'd done wrong, but I didn't even know what my crime was.

The God I'd experienced growing up was like that. Angry, vengeful, impossible to please. Smiting people dead for small infractions, like touching the Ark of the Covenant or telling a lie. As I attended church during grad school, I'd gotten a more holistic picture of God that was more like a concerned parent than an insane dictator, but the way I felt after my cancer diagnosis made me wonder if my first impression of God was more accurate.

My friend Stephan called me shortly after my diagnosis to see how I was doing. He said that afternoon he'd gone to Whole Foods to get a protein shake. As he was paying for it, the cashier asked if he'd like to make a donation to breast cancer research and have a pink ribbon with his name on it mounted on the wall. "No thanks," he said, and collected his change.

When he got to his car, he thought about everything I was going through, and he walked back into the store and bought a ribbon. The cashier asked for his name so she could write it on the ribbon.

"Just write, 'Jesus Loves Sarah,'" he said. I was speechless when he told me that.

"Jesus does love you, you know," Stephan said.

I nodded silently, skeptically. Because cancer felt like the antithesis of love.

"Sarah," he said gently, "God isn't mad at you. He is madly in love with you."

That night as I tried to fall asleep in the dark, I felt anxiety rising in me, and I knew I was about to have a panic attack. I started to repeat what Stephan had told me. Over and over again I whispered the words, *Jesus loves Sarah. Jesus loves Sarah. Jesus loves Sarah.*

But I didn't believe them.

CHAPTER THIRTY-THREE

I SPENT THE FIRST week after my cancer diagnosis trying to explain to my family and friends and coworkers how I felt and what I needed them to do, and what I needed them not to say. I got tired of explaining, and soon I was talking to Libby instead. She understood like no one else what it was like to have cancer and stare down the barrel of treatment and wonder if you had what it took to get through it.

"Whatever it takes," Libby told me over and over. "Just do whatever it takes to survive."

Libby came to visit me in the hospital after my surgery, and called me every week that summer, just to make sure I was okay. And then, three months before Christmas, her cancer came back. It had metastasized to her ribs and her liver and her brain. She had surgery, and then endless rounds of chemo and radiation.

After my medical leave was up, I resumed classes at Columbia. Every week I took the train to Manhattan for class. After class I took the subway to Libby's neighborhood on the Upper West Side, bought two slices of vegetarian pizza and two Cokes, and took the elevator to the tenth floor of her apartment building, where she and her little terrier Bob were always waiting for me.

While we ate our pizza, we talked about relationships. She told me how she fell in love with the man who was now her husband. They'd been coworkers, and then, when she was diagnosed with cancer, he showed up at her first chemo session to keep her company. They started dating, and soon after were engaged and then married.

I told her Ian was the opposite. We'd been nearly engaged, but since I came home from the hospital, he'd backed away. He took days to return my phone calls and e-mails. When I asked why he was so distant, he shrugged and blamed his absence on work. I told him how badly I missed and needed him, but nothing changed.

"Everyone handles cancer in their own way," Libby said. "Give Ian as much space as he needs right now. He'll come around."

As she was talking, I wondered, *Why does Ian get to handle cancer his way? Why can't he handle it my way, since I'm the one who's sick?*

When we'd exhausted the topic of men, we'd discuss writing and cancer treatments and chemo side effects. It was a relief to be able to talk to someone who really understood what it was like, without offering apologies or feeling pressured to hyperspiritualize the experience of cancer.

Unlike what some people from my church tried to tell me, cancer was not a gift from God; it was more like a demon that had escaped from hell.

As Christmas grew closer that year, Libby and I started talking even more. Her cancer wasn't responding to treatments this time, and she was terrified of dying. My cancer was gone, but the scars on my chest ached continually, and kept me awake most nights. The sleep deprivation and sadness dragged me further down every day, until I was desperately low.

A few days before Christmas, I walked out of my apartment building and a man with a press pass and a camera stepped in front of me. He introduced himself as a reporter for the local newspaper.

"Any thoughts on what transpired here today?" he asked. I told him I wasn't aware that anything had happened.

He pointed to the parking lot next to the apartment building, where several police cars and an ambulance had gathered, their lights flashing.

"I didn't hear anything," I told him. "What happened?"

"A graduate student jumped off the top of your building and committed suicide," he said. As I walked to work, I considered the student who had jumped from the roof. It was such a simple, fast way to die, and my first thought was, *Why didn't I think of that?*

CHAPTER THIRTY-FOUR

THE WEEK AFTER I helped Hadhi open the mail and heard more about the Monster, I went over to the apartment to drop off some more supplies. As Hadhi answered the door, she brushed tears from her eyes and gave me a limp hug.

After all she'd been through, and after all we'd talked about—violence in Somalia, her abusive husband, the deaths of her three sons—I had never seen her cry. So when I saw the tears that evening, my heart sank. Something must be really, really wrong.

"Hadhi, what's the matter?" I asked as she locked the deadbolt behind us and turned to face me.

The apartment was freezing again, and even though it was night, there was only one light on in the whole apartment.

"No money, Sarah," she said. "No money. I no make the lights, I no make the heat. And tomorrow I no make the phone."

I asked Fahari to translate, and she explained that they were out of money. The landlord was threatening to evict them if they couldn't pay the rent in twenty-four hours. The cell phone had been cut off because Hadhi was behind in the payments. And if she couldn't pay the electric bill soon, the power company was going to shut off the lights and the heat.

I was too sad—and too tired—to cry.

I'd spent hundreds of dollars buying clean clothes, groceries, and cleaning supplies for this struggling family. I went to the apartment a few times a week and helped the girls with their homework, taught Hadhi how to cook with American appliances, and sang the girls to sleep.

I realized as I looked into Hadhi's desperate eyes that in spite of everything I'd tried to do for them, they were still on the brink of disaster. They were still about to slip through the cracks, and the safety net I'd tried to construct for them could not hold their weight.

Hadhi explained that the next morning she was going to go to DHS while the older girls were at school, to beg for more money to pay the utilities. I didn't know what use I could be to her, but I at least wanted to show that she had a friend who cared about what was happening to her and her family.

So I asked if I could go with her. She nodded slowly, and her shoulders sank in resignation. "Yah, Sahara, yah," she said.

Before I left that night, I took all the cash from my wallet and gave it to Hadhi. "Turn the heat on," I urged her. "The girls are cold."

The morning after Hadhi told me about their financial problems, I borrowed Karina's car seats and drove over to the apartment. I helped her dress Chaki and Lelo, and we loaded them into my car and started driving. I didn't realize until we were on the road that there were multiple DHS offices in Portland. I thought Hadhi might be able to point me in the right direction, but she was used to tending to the girls while they rode the bus, and had no idea how to get to "The Office," as she called it.

I knew of a DHS office near the train stop where I'd first met the family, so I decided to drive there for starters. We drove for about twenty minutes, and I pulled into the parking lot. "Is this the office?"

I asked Hadhi. She looked confused. "No office," she said, shaking her head.

If this wasn't the right DHS office, at least the people working at this one could point us in the right direction, I thought. So Hadhi and I got the two girls out of their car seats, and the four of us walked inside. The twenty-something-year-old guy who was working at the reception desk looked up Hadhi's case in the computer, and then printed a map of the DHS office closest to her house, where he said her case had initially been opened.

While we were driving back the way we'd come, I thought about meeting Hadhi and the girls on that first afternoon. I'd often wondered what the odds were of our chance encounter, considering how many factors had to be aligned for us to get on the same train at the same time. Now that I knew more about their lives, I was even more puzzled. If it wasn't close to their house or their DHS office or their doctor's office or any grocery stores, what were they doing at my stop that day?

CHAPTER THIRTY-FIVE

T HE NIGHT THE grad student jumped off the top of my apartment building, Libby called with more bad news. Her cancer had progressed, and her doctors told her she'd exhausted all of her treatment options.

"You're the pastor's kid, you tell me why this is happening. Isn't God supposed to show us love and compassion and shit like that?"

"Well, I used to think so but now I don't know," I answered honestly. "I mean, I wouldn't wish cancer on someone I hated, let alone someone I loved."

She told me she was going to pull the covers over her head and binge on Cheetos. "Merry fucking Christmas," she said as she hung up.

The next night, I went to a holiday party with Ian. It had been a few weeks since I'd seen him, and I was relieved to find that he was his old self—warm and funny and affectionate. He interlaced his fingers with mine as we mingled with the other party guests.

During the course of the evening, two of my friends announced they were moving out of state, and another friend announced she was pregnant. I overheard her telling someone that she knew she was pregnant because "all of a sudden my boobs got really big."

I tried to be sociable and engaging, but I couldn't do it. "We have to go," I told Ian as I tugged on his hand. We said a hurried good-bye and walked down the street to his apartment. He put water on for tea while I went to hang up my coat. A few minutes later he found me sitting in the closet, crying.

"What's the matter?" he asked.

"My friends are leaving me," I sobbed.

He pulled me close to him and rested his chin on the top of my head. "It's okay," he said. "I'll be here."

"And my friend knew she was pregnant because her boobs got big."

"What?" he asked with a laugh.

"I may not ever get pregnant, and my boobs are gone—they'll never be big," I cried.

"I love you anyway," he said.

I kept crying. Finally I was able to get the words out. "And Libby's dying," I wailed.

He gave up and conceded, "And Libby's dying."

CHAPTER THIRTY-SIX

A FEW DAYS AFTER my closet meltdown, I flew home to Chicago. My parents and siblings picked me up from the airport, and we drove to church for the Christmas Eve service.

I had always hoped I'd be like Mary. As the preacher's daughter, I had played Mary in our church's annual Christmas pageant many times. I had no doubt that, like Mary, I would be a young woman who loved God, whose life took an extraordinary turn.

My life *had* taken an extraordinary turn, but in the wrong direction. Instead of beating the odds to become pregnant with the Messiah, I'd beaten million-to-one odds and gotten breast cancer in my twenties. And God was nowhere to be found.

At the end of the Christmas Eve service, the ushers dimmed the lights and passed out small white candles. As I held the flickering light in my hand, we began to sing Christmas carols.

Angels we have heard on high,
Sweetly singing o'er the plains,
And the mountains in reply
Echoing their joyous strain.
Gloria, in excelsis Deo!

In excelsis Deo. I knew from my Sunday school days that the phrase was Latin for "God in the highest." It reminded me of another Latin phrase, *in extremis.* This was a phrase I had learned in my medical training that described a patient who was struggling to breathe as they died. *In extremis* is translated as "in the farthest reaches" or "at the point of death."

As I listened to people around me singing carols, I thought, *God, I don't want You to be in the highest; I need You to be with me now in the lowest.*

That's where I felt that Christmas: In the lowest depths. In the farthest reaches. At the point of death. My mastectomy was in May, and since then I'd been in a deep depression. Instead of feeling better, I continued to feel worse—and December was the worst month yet.

Ian and a few other friends had thrown a dinner party two weeks before Christmas to celebrate my birthday.

When they brought out the cake, I closed my eyes, leaned over the candles, and made a wish. Actually, it was more like a prayer. *Please, God, please don't let this year be any worse than last year was. I can't take any more.*

For months now I'd felt like someone very close to me had died, and no matter how honestly and deeply I grieved, the sadness wouldn't lift. No matter how hard I tried, I couldn't shake the darkness. At the suggestion of my oncologist, I joined an online breast cancer support group in the hopes of finding a community to encourage me while I recovered from the physical and emotional scars. I chatted with women who had walked this road, and I begged them to tell me what to do to get past this pain.

One woman told me she'd been depressed after her mastectomy, too. Her Kabbalah instructor told her to write an obituary for her breasts, and let them go. After we'd chatted for a while, she wrote, "Honey, go write that obit and have a good cry."

But in that moment, I wasn't sad; I was angry. Write an obituary? If I did that, the loss would be irrevocable. Say good-bye? I had spent the past few months telling God how unacceptable this loss was, how He needed to appeal His decision and give me back my breasts and my health and my life. If I said good-bye, I would cement my loss, and God might think I was okay.

I was definitely not okay. I went from being nearly engaged to Ian to seeing him every other week, if I was lucky. He blamed his absence on work, but I couldn't help wondering what the real reason was. Was he seeing someone else? Was he less attracted to this scarred, sad version of the Sarah he'd once loved? Regardless of the reason, I grieved the expanding distance between us. I spent hours a day sitting on the couch in my studio apartment, staring at the sky while tears ran down my face.

And so as I thought about my birthday wish, I told God He didn't have to make my life better right away; I could probably survive as long as it didn't get any worse. I blew out the candles, but before I could open my eyes, people around the table started screaming and I smelled smoke. As I looked up to see what was happening, Ian yelled, "Your hair's on fire!"

He dumped water on his hand, then grabbed a fistful of my hair and squelched the flames. As my nostrils filled with the stench of burnt hair and my friends scurried to clean up the mess, I thought, *If your hair catches on fire while you're making a wish, does that mean it isn't coming true?*

CHAPTER THIRTY-SEVEN

WHEN HADHI AND I finally arrived at the right DHS office, we waited in line for about fifteen minutes until we were able to talk to the receptionist. I told her I'd come with the family to find out what their benefits were and what we could do to pay their utilities. She directed us to take a number from a red dispenser mounted on the wall, and then we sat down in a bank of chairs to wait our turn.

I had never been inside a DHS office, but I'd been to plenty of DMVs, and it was pretty much the same. Take a number, sit down in a row of chairs, watch for your number to appear on a little black box on the wall, approach an official-looking worker at a small window.

And then beg for mercy.

After we took a number, we waited. And waited. And waited. Hadhi sat next to me in silence while Lelo sat in my lap, and Chaki crawled on the floor under the chairs.

As we waited, the room filled up with dozens and dozens of Invisibles. Broken teeth, deep wrinkles, greasy hair, ill-fitting clothes. They all seemed to belong together, and to understand each other. I

was the one who was out of place here. I wondered if they felt as uncomfortable in my world as I felt in theirs.

Lelo had brought her dice, or as she called it, "my game," which
kept her busy for a while. But eventually her game got old, and she
and Chaki started getting bored. There was no TV, no magazines, no
books, no toys. Just chairs and cubicles.

"Do you want to sing a song?" I asked her.

Lelo nodded, and began singing a song the older girls had picked
up at school.

One, two, buckle my shoe,
Three, four, shut the door,
Five, six, pick up sticks,
Seven, eight, shut the gate,
Nine, ten, do it again.

We sang it together quietly, over and over and over again, until
our number came up, and we made our way to the next open cubicle.

A tall, thin man with white hair that fell to his shoulders sat on
the other side of the cubicle. Before we arrived at DHS, I'd imagined
that I would have to be a tough advocate for the family in the face of
indifferent, jaded state workers. But this man, who introduced himself as Paul, wasn't indifferent at all. He had a warm smile, and gently
asked Hadhi for the information to look up her case file.

Hadhi had showed me the paperwork she had kept from previous
visits to DHS, so I knew that in the past month, their cash assistance
had been decreased by $130 per month, without any explanation.
She'd been able to scrape together enough money to cover the rent.
If we could get the $130 reinstated, it would cover their utilities, I
told Paul.

He explained that because the father had moved out, their household had gone from seven people to six, and their assistance had been decreased accordingly. Usually in that case, the state goes after the father for child support. But the Department of Justice had decided the family was safer if the father didn't know where they were, so the petition for child support had been dropped.

While we waited to see if there was any way to appeal this or get any extra assistance, Lelo got antsy.

"Another song?" she asked.

"Sure," I said. "What should we sing?"

"'The Happy Song'!" she said with a smile, referring to the song I'd taught her and her sisters a few weeks before.

I started singing:

If you're happy and you know it, clap your hands,
If you're happy and you know it, clap your hands,
If you're happy and you know it, then your face will surely show it,
If you're happy and you know it, clap your hands.

She and Chaki clapped enthusiastically, and we sang it again. On the next round, I heard people waiting in the chairs behind us start to sing with us, and clap along with the girls.

Before we'd finished, half of the Invisibles in the waiting room were smiling and singing:

If you're happy and you know it, then your face will surely show it...

Paul came back with the bad news that there wasn't anything else DHS could do for the family. After they paid the rent each month, there was about $50 left over to cover all their other expenses. It wouldn't be enough to keep the heat on for the winter, but the only thing we could do was to approach nonprofits and ask for assistance.

"We'll figure something out," I promised Hadhi as we got the girls bundled up in their coats and prepared to leave.

CHAPTER THIRTY-EIGHT

A FEW MONTHS AFTER my hair caught on fire, I sat with Ian on a beach in Mexico on Easter Sunday. It was almost exactly one year after my diagnosis and mastectomy, and we decided to take a vacation before I took the next step in my cancer recovery, which was reconstructive surgery on my chest.

During the mastectomy, after the surgeon removed all my breast tissue, a plastic surgeon had come into the OR and inserted temporary saline implants called expanders under the skin before they sutured the incisions closed. The expanders were like implants, but they started out flat and were injected with a little bit of saline over time so the skin could have time to expand before the permanent saline implants were inserted.

When I met with my plastic surgeon for the initial consultation before the mastectomy, he told me he was going to make me a 34C.

"You realize I only weigh 105 pounds, right?" I said. "If you make me too big, I'll look like Dolly Parton."

"You won't look ridiculous. You'll be a knockout, like a breast cancer Barbie. Besides," he added, "anything less than a 34C would be a waste of my time."

He was brash, but he was one of Yale's top plastic surgeons, so I agreed to his plan. But the promise of future beauty didn't make up for the present pain. A few times a month for the past year I'd gone to the plastic surgeon's office and lain down on the table while he inserted a needle through my skin and into the rubber port, and then filled the expanders with saline until the skin over my chest was taut.

Normal breast tissue lies between the chest wall muscles and the skin, but they place the expanders underneath the muscle against the ribs so if new tumors grow, they can be more easily detected because they would be on top of the implant rather than underneath it. While it is a logical medical practice, it is an excruciating experience.

After the first expansion, I went home and tried to get comfortable. I tried sitting in a chair, lying down on the couch, lying in bed, soaking in a hot bath. But nothing I did assuaged the pain of the chest muscles being pulled off my rib cage, and of the overlying tight skin being stretched to its limit. If I breathed too deeply or moved the wrong way, the muscles would go into spasm, making me feel like I was being suffocated by a vise grip around my torso.

My surgeon had told me the process would be mildly uncomfortable, and I was worried that if I complained about the pain or asked for a prescription for muscle relaxants or narcotics, he would think I was a drug seeker.

So I didn't ask for anything. Instead, after each subsequent expansion, Ian took me to a bar and bought me a Long Island iced tea. And then he drove me home and dropped me off, where I napped until the alcohol had worn off, and then spent the rest of the night sobbing in pain.

I spent a year trying to decide which was worse: the physical or the emotional pain. I hadn't counted on the grief I would feel after my surgery, and I had no idea how much I would resent my post-mastectomy body.

I wasn't just sad; I was *angry*. Angry at God for disrupting my life. Angry at myself for not being more resilient. And most of all, I was angry at my body for betraying me. While I'd been going to college and grad school and spending time with friends and serving at church and enjoying my life, my body had been plotting to kill me.

CHAPTER THIRTY-NINE

IAN AND I HADN'T talked about getting married since my cancer diagnosis the year before, but we were still dating. Kind of. He drove me to most of my doctors' appointments, and we watched a movie or went out to dinner a few times a month. It wasn't an ideal relationship, but it was enough. At that point, I didn't need a fancy white gown or an expensive Tiffany diamond. I was content to have someone familiar and caring to keep me company. Ian was the last remnant of my previous life, and being with him reminded me of the funny, intelligent, loving girl I'd been. And maybe, I thought, maybe if I could remember who I'd been, I could be her again.

While Ian and I lay side by side on chaise lounges on the beach in Cancun sipping piña coladas, I thought about the hell the last year had been, and the surgery I was scheduled to have a few days after I got home from this trip. Just thinking about all of it made me feel too weary for words.

Before my mastectomy, I'd had so much faith. But as the months dragged on with no hope of relief in sight, I felt like I was drifting further and further away from God. Or was He drifting from me? It was hard to tell who left whom, but the distance was unmistakable.

The only time I prayed now was at bedtime while I was falling asleep. I felt so estranged from Him that every night I asked Him to take me to heaven in my sleep, because I couldn't find Him anywhere on earth.

I thought maybe now that I was in a different country, I could get through to Him. Maybe if I spoke in Spanish, I'd be even more likely to reach Him. I only knew a few phrases that I'd learned on the job while working in a Hispanic medical clinic, so it was a pretty short prayer. *"No mas, Señor. Por favor, no mas."* I needed God to know that I was maxed out. I couldn't take any more grief, any more scars, any more loss.

How do you say "uncle" in Spanish? I wondered.

We took a walk along the beach before dinner that evening. Ian was wearing khaki pants and an untucked white-collared shirt, and I was wearing a sleeveless blue sundress. He asked another couple on the beach to take a picture of us, and we stood side by side with our arms wrapped around each other's waists and smiled.

After he tucked the camera in his pocket, Ian put his hands on my hips and pulled me close to him, until my head was resting on his chest. We stood there, silently, watching brilliant colors light up the twilight sky. When the sunset was over, he whispered, "It's been a long year."

I nodded.

"I've missed you," he said, his voice breaking.

"It's almost over," I said, lifting my eyes to meet his teary gaze. "One more surgery, and it will all be over."

CHAPTER FORTY

O NE EVENING IN THE middle of November, Hadhi and I sat in the hallway drinking Somali coffee as the girls slept in the room next door. She told me they'd be celebrating Eid the following day—or as she explained it, Somali Christmas.

She explained that she used to buy the girls presents for Eid. "But this year, no money," she said as she shrugged and flashed a weary smile. Then she noticed that I was wearing triangle-shaped silver earrings embedded with little round crystals. She reached her hand up and fingered my right earring.

"Beautiful," she said. "I wear these for Eid?"

"Of course," I said.

I took them off and handed them to her, and as she put them on, she told me in broken English that if she couldn't buy her girls presents, at least she could look nice while she cooked curried goat and rice for them.

That night when I got home, I read a little bit about the holiday. I had grown up in Sunday school, so I knew the Judeo-Christian story where God asked Abraham to sacrifice his son Isaac. Just as Abraham was getting ready to make the sacrifice, an angel stopped him.

Then Abraham found a ram to sacrifice instead, and so his son's life was spared. It was the same story my parents had remembered the night of my sister's heart surgery, when they relinquished control of my siblings and me.

Eid celebrated the same story, but with different characters. In the story of Eid, it was Allah who asked Abraham to sacrifice his other son, Ishmael. But similarly, Allah stopped Abraham before he killed Ishmael, and blessed Abraham for his act of obedience and faith.

By the time Eid rolled around, I had been blogging about the Invisible Girls for a few months. A pastor of a nearby church found the blog and contacted me to tell me they wanted to donate supplies from their food bank to help feed the family. The morning after I gave Hadhi my earrings, I drove to the church and the pastor loaded up my car with frozen chicken, rice, dried lentils, frozen vegetables, and juice.

On the night of Eid, I drove over to the apartment and told the girls I had a surprise for them in my car. They put on their flip-flops and came tripping out into the parking lot to see what I had in my car. I opened the back and showed them the boxes of food. They started jumping up and down, squealing with joy.

I loaded up their arms, and they went running back and forth between my car and the apartment, unloading the supplies. When the car was mostly emptied, Abdallah noticed a bag of underwear and socks I'd bought to give them as Eid gifts.

Since I met the family, I'd been trying to find the balance of helping them without undermining Hadhi's role as the family's provider, and without making the family permanently dependent on free handouts. But since Eid was equivalent to Christmas, it seemed appropriate to give them each a small gift.

"This is for us?" Abdallah whispered, looking up at me hopefully. I smiled and grabbed the bag and brought it inside with us.

After we'd put the food away, we sat in a circle on the living room floor. I opened the bag and pulled out socks and underwear for all of them. They were so excited, they put the underwear on over their clothes and strutted around the living room.

Chaki put her hand on her hip and said, "I cute! I cute!"

The older girls ran around the living room to try out their new socks. Every time they ran past me, they'd hold out their covered feet and ask, "What word is this?"

"Socks," I said. They repeated the word while they chased one another around the apartment.

As I watched Hadhi sitting on the floor smiling, absently playing with her earrings while watching her girls enjoying their Somali Christmas, I thought about the story of Eid. It was interesting that three diverse religions told a similar story, as if to prove the universal constant that the greatest sacrifice God could demand of his followers was to ask them to give up their children.

The Christian tradition says that God saved Abraham from sacrificing his son, and then a few thousand years later, God sent His own son, Jesus, to the world. But God did not spare Himself the ultimate pain; instead, He allowed Jesus to give His life to atone for the world's sin.

Hadhi was one of the most selfless parents I knew. She'd given up her homeland, her extended family, her friends, and her familiar life in Somalia to give her girls a chance for a better life. She was trusting enough to let me be a part of her family's fabric, and humble enough to learn a million little details about how to run a household in America. Hadhi's sacrifices and her attention to even the slightest details—like the earrings she wore to help her girls celebrate Eid—showed me how universally relentless a parent's love is.

On that cold November evening, my heart warmed as I witnessed how Hadhi loved her girls. How Abraham loved Isaac and Ishmael. How God loved the world.

CHAPTER FORTY-ONE

A FEW DAYS AFTER I got back from Mexico, I had reconstructive surgery on my chest. My surgeon took out the expanders that had tortured me for the past year and inserted permanent saline implants. I remember being concerned that he would see how tan I was from lying in the Mexico sun for a few days, and scold me for not wearing enough sunscreen.

Instead, my surgeon called me two days after the surgery, while I was groggy from pain medication and not-very-restful sleep. But I caught enough of the conversation to rally my brain to comprehend the words, "We found a mass on the chest muscle in surgery...the biopsy results are back...you have cancer."

Again. I have cancer *again,* I wanted to correct the surgeon. I hung up the phone, and I thought, *God, that's enough. Having cancer one time is an accident. It could happen to anyone. But having cancer twice? Well, that's cancer on* purpose.

My mom flew out from Illinois, and took me to my oncology appointment that week. My oncologist told me that because I was so young, and my cancer had recurred so quickly, I needed the most aggressive treatment they had. The treatment plan included more surgery to remove all the cancer from my chest wall, two different kinds of chemo, and thirty treatments of radiation.

I thought about what the chemo and radiation would do to my fertility. "Can I freeze my eggs before I start treatment?" I asked.

He shook his head, and explained they'd have to give me hormones to stimulate my ovaries in order to harvest the eggs, but those hormones could fuel the cancer cells, which had tested estrogen receptor-positive. "I'm really sorry," he said. "But losing your fertility is just a risk we'll have to take."

It took another week to get everything scheduled, and in that space I begged God to let me die.

Just take me home, I pleaded every night. *I can't do this anymore, just take me home.*

But He took Libby instead.

The night before I started chemo, I got an e-mail from the dean of the journalism school saying that Libby had died, and her funeral was in three days.

I didn't make the funeral because I was vomiting on the bathroom floor and my hair was falling out in clumps. I was far too sick to take a ninety-minute train ride from New Haven to Manhattan.

And so I never got to tell Libby good-bye. The last e-mail I got from her was two weeks before, when I'd written to tell her about my cancer recurrence. The e-mail she sent back was filled with misspellings and randomly capitalized words. She had been such a meticulous writer and editor, I guessed from the mistakes that the cancerous tumors in her brain were affecting her cognition.

The last sentence she wrote to me was, "Cancer is fucking cruel and sick." And as I lay on the cold tile bathroom floor vomiting over and over again the night of my first chemo treatment, I agreed.

CHAPTER FORTY-TWO

Every time I visited the Somali family, I learned something new about them. At first it was obvious physical things, like the fact that they didn't have toilet paper, or that Hadhi didn't know how to work the oven or turn on the heat. But once those external things had been addressed, I started learning about their internal experiences of America.

It took me awhile to recognize, and then admit to myself, that because their language skills were poor and they were unable to communicate complicated concepts through words, I often assumed that their thought process was as simple as their speech. And then I realized that this wasn't just true for the Somali family; it was true for many indigent populations. It was easy for me to make the atrocious assumption that because they couldn't articulate sadness, helplessness, discouragement, or other emotions in English, they must not feel them.

But the Invisible Girls, as I began to call them, were a constant reminder that their minds were just as sharp and their hearts just as sensitive as anyone's. And they were just as overwhelmed and confused by their new environment as I would be if I were dropped into Somalia without any advance warning.

I didn't realize how much they didn't know about American culture until I went over to their apartment one evening and was greeted by Hadhi, who opened the door and thrust her cell phone at me. A male was on the other end speaking English, and she had no idea what he was saying.

"Hello?" I said as I took the phone.

"Nine-one-one, what's your emergency?" he said, sounding annoyed.

I looked around. No one was bleeding, and nothing was on fire. "I think we must have called you by accident," I said. "There's no emergency here."

"Someone called from this number and hung up," he said.

"I'm sorry, I'll have a talk with them," I said, and hung up.

The girls were all sitting on a mattress in the living room, giggling. I sat down in front of them. "Did you guys call nine-one-one on your mom's cell phone?" I asked.

Instead of trying to deny what they'd done, they nodded vigorously, taking full credit. "Why?" I asked.

Fahari explained they'd learned about 911 in school that day, and they wanted to find out if the number worked, and what happened when you called it.

I gave them a stern lecture about not calling 911 unless there was an emergency.

"Understand?" I asked.

They nodded.

Fahari said they had another question for me. The other day when they came home from school, they'd found a pizza advertisement hanging on their front doorknob. "We called the number and asked for a pizza," Fahari said. "And then the man came over with pizza and got very angry and took the pizza away."

"Well, did you pay him for it?"

She looked puzzled. "You have to pay?" she asked.

They had assumed that every time you called the number on the flyer, someone showed up with a free pizza. No wonder they were so excited about America. In their minds, it was literally a magical place.

Hadhi had bought old VHS tapes of Disney movies for 25 cents at Goodwill. After seeing the movie *Bambi*, the girls were convinced that all the animals in America could talk.

After watching *Mary Poppins*, they asked me to teach them how to snap their fingers. The two littlest girls didn't have the fine motor skills necessary to do this, but the older girls figured it out quickly. Fahari walked around the apartment reaching her hand into closets and cupboards, snapping her fingers. She came back to me in the living room and said, "It no work."

"What doesn't work?" I asked her.

She explained that in the movie, every time the nanny or the kids snapped their fingers, the room got magically cleaned. "Maybe it only works for white people?" she asked hesitantly.

CHAPTER FORTY-THREE

T HE LONGER THE Invisible Girls were in the United States, the more self-conscious they became. They realized they dressed and spoke differently than other children. Fahari, Abdallah, and Sadaka constantly struggled for acceptance at school, and often acted out at home because they couldn't get it.

On the evening of the 911 incident, I caught Fahari taking my iPod and some lip gloss out of my purse. "Fahari! What are you doing?" I asked.

She froze. "I was going to give these to girls at school," she said.

Likely story, I thought as I made her apologize and put the items back.

She pouted for a few minutes, and then, like a passing storm cloud, her mood shifted. She took a notebook and a pen out of her backpack, and came and sat down on the living room floor next to me. "Can you help me write notes to kids at my school?" she asked. Thinking this would be great English practice for her, I agreed to help.

"What do you want the notes to say?"

"Can you write, *Please don't be mean to me. I need a friend. I'm just like you*"? she said.

I stopped writing and looked up. "Fahari, how does school make you feel?"

Her big brown eyes welled up with sorrow, and she leaned her head on my shoulder as tears began to spill down her cheeks. I pulled her closer to me, and sat with her in silence as she wept.

After the fear of not being able to pay the rent, the hours spent at the DHS office trying to figure out why their benefits were cut, dwindling food stamps, and the concern over the electric bill, there were still more dilemmas.

A few days after I helped Fahari write notes to her classmates, Hadhi called me, and she sounded panicked. She was talking hurriedly in Somali, but I recognized the words "Chaki—fever—hospital."

"You have to take Chaki to the hospital?" I asked.

"Yah, Sarah, you come? You come my house now?"

"I'm on my way," I said.

On my way over to the house, I stopped at a department store to buy two car seats so I could drive Hadhi and the two smallest girls in my car. When I'd driven them before, I'd borrowed Karina's car seats, but it seemed like a good investment to have some of my own now, and we'd need them to drive to the hospital.

I went to the children's section of the department store—the one with cribs and strollers and bottles and bibs and car seats. It was an aisle I avoided as much as possible, because it was a painful reminder of my infertility—*the parts I'll never use, the children I'll never have.*

But today was easier because as I looked at car seats, I wasn't thinking about myself; I was thinking of Lelo and Chaki. There were two fabric patterns to choose from. One was black and gray; the other model was pink and purple with small doll figures on it. I bought two of the pink and purple booster seats, installed them in the backseat of my car, and drove to the apartment.

When I arrived, I found that the older girls had left for school. Hadhi was getting Lelo ready in the bedroom while Chaki lay on a mattress in the living room. She was dressed in an ankle-length skirt, Muslim headdress, and a tie-dyed T-shirt that read JOE'S CRAB SHACK.

Hadhi explained that Chaki had been running a fever for a few days, and today was refusing to eat. Hadhi had already made an appointment at the free clinic, but needed a ride to get there.

"It's no problem, I'll take you," I said.

I picked Chaki up and held her on my lap while we waited for her mom and sister to get ready. There was no thermometer to tell exactly how high her fever was, but I could tell from her skin temperature and flushed cheeks that she was burning up.

She lay limply in my arms and looked up at me, asking me random questions with slightly slurred speech, as if she were inebriated. "Sahara," she said. Then she started again, "Sahara, you like my shirt?"

"Yes, baby," I said. "I love your shirt."

"Sahara? Sahara? Do you have any *lings*?" she asked, using the Somali word for "oranges."

"Not today," I said. "No lings today."

"Sahara?" she asked, almost asleep now.

"Yes, baby?"

"Sahara, do you have a boy?"

She fell asleep before I could answer. I kissed her forehead and held her for a few more minutes, until everyone was ready to leave.

CHAPTER FORTY-FOUR

Before I started chemo, my blond hair was halfway down my back. I thought it would be traumatic and messy to let the long strands fall out slowly during chemo, and I didn't want my hair to go to waste, so I decided to cut it and donate it to Locks of Love.

Three of my friends drove me to a hair salon, then produced a bottle of champagne and four glasses. We toasted to my hair, and then a kind, tearful hairdresser cut it off. I was left with a short pixie cut, the shortest haircut I'd ever had in my life.

That evening I was meeting Ian and some other friends for dinner. Ian was the last to arrive, and I stood up as he made his way to the table. It was the first time he'd seen me with hair this short.

I went to hug him, but he took my shoulders and held me at arm's length, inspecting my new look. I was so afraid and so self-conscious, I just wanted him to hug me and tell me that my hair didn't matter, that he loved me anyway, that we were going to get through this.

Instead he said, "Whoa. You look like a boy. This is going to take some getting used to." And as he let go of me, my heart sank at his tepid response.

My mom stayed with me while I went through the first round

of treatments. We lived together in my tiny studio apartment, and every night she slept on a mat on the floor next to my bed.

After two rounds of chemo, I woke up one morning to find clumps of hair on my pillow. I decided that rather than wait for it all to fall out, looking like a diseased Chia Pet in the process, I would shave it all off. But I was too weak to stand up in front of the mirror, so later that morning I ended up sitting on the lid of the toilet in the bathroom while my mom slathered my head in shaving cream, then took a razor and shaved my head to the skin.

When she'd finished, I stood in front of the bathroom mirror, looking for any traces that the girl staring back at me now was somehow a part of the girl I used to know. But I couldn't find her anywhere. I didn't recognize this pale, bald creature with dark circles under her eyes.

I thought of Samson and Delilah. When Delilah learned that Samson's hair was the source of his strength, she chopped it off while he was sleeping and rendered him powerless. As I studied my reflection in the mirror, it occurred to me that maybe Samson's hair wasn't his *source* of strength; maybe it was a *symbol* of his strength. And maybe when Delilah cut off his hair, he didn't lose his power because he lost his hair; he just woke up the next morning and looked in the mirror, and suddenly for the life of him couldn't remember who he was.

It wasn't just my head that was unfamiliar; I also didn't recognize my chest. The week after my surgeon found the recurrence, I'd had a second surgery to remove the rest of the cancerous tumor on my chest wall. During that operation the surgeon had removed my right saline implant so I could have radiation on that side after I finished chemo. I eyed my bald head and one-breasted chest and wondered, *Who is that freak?*

Ian asked if he could take me out that afternoon. As I put on my bra and stuffed the right cup with a pair of rolled-up athletic socks, I fought back the urge to loathe myself. "It's okay," I said as I forced myself to take deep breaths. "It's not forever; it's just for now. You won't be bald forever, you're only bald for now. Your breast isn't gone forever; it's only gone for now."

When Ian picked me up, I asked what we were going to do for the afternoon.

"I thought we could get coffee," he said. We drove ten minutes to Starbucks, but instead of parking the car so we could walk in, or getting in line behind the other cars in the drive-thru, he pulled into a parking spot and left the car running.

Without taking off his seat belt, he turned to me and said, "I can't do this anymore. It's just too hard."

I opened my mouth but no sound came out. It was like I'd been kicked so hard in the stomach I couldn't speak—not because I was in incomprehensible pain, but because I'd been deprived of all my air.

I wanted to scream at God for giving me more pain than any one person should have been expected to handle. I wanted to curse Him for taking my last piece of hope.

I wanted to yell at the universe for its unfairness. How was it that Ian could choose to tap out, but I couldn't? Why couldn't I take cancer to Starbucks and say, "Look, I'm sorry, I can't do this. It's just too hard."

I wanted to beat Ian until his body was in as much pain as my soul. And then I wanted to bargain with him, reason with him, convince him to stay. *I'm worth loving. I'm worth fighting for. I'm worth something. Tell me I'm worth something, anything, to you.*

But instead, I sat there in the passenger seat of the idling car, motionless and speechless. In college I'd read a short story about a woman who was murdered. During the attack, she refused to close her eyes. Instead, she kept them open and stared at her attacker, thinking, *You can kill me, but you'll have to look me in the eye while you do it.*

I thought about that woman as I sat there, holding Ian's gaze. *You can rip out my heart, but you'll have to look me in the eye while you do it.*

After a minute of intense silence, he looked away and asked, "Do you want coffee?"

I shook my head. He ordered himself a caramel macchiato at the drive-thru window, and then he drove me home. When we got to my apartment, neither of us said anything. No good-byes. No kisses, no hugs, no tears. Nothing. I climbed out of the car and stood on the sidewalk and watched as the man who was holding my heart drove away.

I hadn't even been gone an hour when I returned to my fourth-floor apartment. My mom was standing in the tiny kitchenette making dinner, and she looked up, surprised to see me back so soon.

"How's Ian?" she asked.

I hesitated for a minute, thinking about how to answer the question. I didn't have the emotional energy to talk about it right now, or to acknowledge the implications of what had just happened. Speaking what was unspeakable was like playing the game KerPlunk—if I pulled out this last stick, all the marbles would come crashing down.

"He's okay," I said. "He said he needs more space." My trite description of our conversation was almost a lie, but at the same time it was almost true. My mom raised one eyebrow, because she knew there was more to it than what I was saying.

I sank into the couch, turned on the TV, and started channel surfing. "It's fine," I said. *Ouch. That was definitely a lie.*

It wasn't until the middle of the night, when my mom was fast asleep on the mattress on the floor near my bed, that I let myself feel the weight of Ian's absence. I remembered him finding me in the closet crying after the party a few months before. "I'll love you anyway," he had promised, holding my face tenderly and brushing away my tears with his thumb. And then my hair caught on fire, and Libby died, and my cancer recurred. And now Ian didn't love me anymore.

My shoulders shook as I tried to swallow the sobs that threatened to wake my mom and give me away. As I replayed our last conversation, what haunted me most was that I would've given anything to spend the rest of my life with Ian. And yet, when he was breaking up with me, he hadn't even put the car in park.

CHAPTER FORTY-FIVE

Two months after I met the Somali family, the older girls came home from school and told me they'd started learning about the American holiday Thanksgiving at school, and asked me to tell them more about it.

The first explanation I thought of—that every year Americans kill 45 million turkeys to celebrate that half of the Pilgrims who came to America didn't die during the first winter—sounded ridiculous. So instead of trying to explain it further, I said, "How would you like to celebrate Thanksgiving with me this year?" They were ecstatic.

Every time I went over to their apartment in the weeks leading up to Thanksgiving, they'd race to get their coats and shoes, yelling, "We go to your house *today*?"

Every time I'd shake my head and say, "Nope, not today."

On the morning of Thanksgiving, my housemate Betsy and I drove over to their apartment to pick them up—we needed two cars to transport the six of them. When we knocked on the door, the girls all came running. Hadhi opened the door and motioned for us to come inside. I held my arms out and called, "Who wants to go to my house today?" They screamed and clambered to get their shoes on.

I brought a bag filled with hats and mittens, and once they had their shoes and coats on, I handed out the items—partly because I thought they might like the thought of getting "dressed up" to come to my place, and partly because they didn't own any winter gear.

We piled into the two cars and drove to my town house. My other housemate, Karrie, had made the turkey, and when Betsy and the family and I got home, a bounty of turkey, stuffing, sweet potatoes, green beans, and bread was waiting for us.

We made each person a plate, then sat together in a circle on a blanket in the living room. We gave a quick thanks for the food and for each of them, and then started eating. Just like the night we ate pasta, the girls tried using forks for a few minutes, and then gave up and used their right hands instead.

Some of the girls ate the new food without question, but Lelo was skeptical. She kept holding up each piece of food and asking, "I can eat *this*?"

I nodded at each morsel and said, "Yes, it's okay to eat that."

Then she'd hold up the next piece. "I can eat *this*?"

Chaki ate well until she caught a glimpse of ice cream in the freezer when I reached in to get some ice cubes. For the rest of the meal, whenever I encouraged her to eat, she looked at me hopefully and raised her eyebrows. "Ice cream?" she asked over and over. "I eat your ice cream?"

When everyone had finished eating, we cleared away the dishes. My friend Karina and her husband, Dan, came over with their two towheaded, blue-eyed little boys, who were three and six. We all ate dessert together, sitting in a big circle on the living room floor. The girls devoured their "bumpkin pie" and vanilla ice cream, and then played together with their new American friends. Some of them colored together at the dining room table, while some played with a wooden dollhouse and chairs that were donated by some families at my church.

When it got dark, we decided to pack everyone up and drive them home. It was getting near the girls' bedtime, and we still had a surprise for them.

CHAPTER FORTY-SIX

W HEN I MOVED to Portland, I began attending a church called Imago Dei. Shortly before I met the Somali family, our pastor had introduced the congregation to something he called Change for a Dollar. When we went up to the front table to take Communion, we were encouraged to put whatever pocket change we had into silver buckets. Each week, the elders took the money and gave it away to someone in our city who was in need.

Two weeks before Thanksgiving, I spoke about the Somali family at church, and the congregation gave more than a thousand dollars to the Change for a Dollar fund that day. I used the donated money to buy everything Hadhi and the girls needed for their sparse apartment—a futon, a reading chair, a rug, clean clothes, closet organizers, more blankets, pillows, bath towels, cleaning supplies, silverware, and food.

To make the new household supplies more exciting, I decided to give everything to the family on Thanksgiving night, like a small-scale version of *Extreme Home Makeover*.

My housemates and Karina and I piled Hadhi and the girls, as well as all of the new supplies, in our cars. We drove the caravan from my house to the apartment, and began to unload everything. It was humbling to watch little girls shriek with excitement over silverware and bath towels.

A few hours later, we'd helped Hadhi clean the kitchen and bathroom with the new cleaning supplies, set up house, bathed the girls, and put everyone in clean clothes. Four of the girls sat together on their new living room rug in their clean pajamas, wrapped up in their fleece blankets, watching *The Incredibles*.

I went into the bedroom to finish putting their clothes into the closet organizers we'd bought for them, and I found six-year-old Sadaka sitting in the corner. She was not her usual giggling self; instead, she had a pained look on her face, and she held a large, ratty Michael Jordan jersey against her cheek.

"You can't keep that shirt," I said as I tried to gently take it from her. "It's stained, and it's way too big for you."

She looked around the room, making sure that her mom and sisters were out of earshot. When she saw that we were alone, she motioned for me to come sit next to her. Then she cupped her hand around my ear, leaned in close, and whispered, "Can I tell you a secret?"

"Of course," I said.

"This shirt is my dad's," she said. "I kept it when he went away." Still holding the jersey, she climbed into my lap, and tears welled up in her big brown eyes.

"Do you miss your daddy?" I asked her.

She nodded, and her tears spilled onto my shirt.

I kissed the top of her head, and held her for a long time, until she'd finished crying. When she was done, she wiped her eyes with her sleeve, then leaned close to my ear and whispered, "Can I tell you another secret?"

"Of course," I said. "You can tell me anything."

"I love you, Sahara."

"I love you too, baby." I hugged her closer. "I love you, too."

As I drove home that night, I thought about the meaning of the original Thanksgiving, how its participants celebrated that natives were willing to help foreign settlers who'd come to a new country without the means of surviving its perils. I thought about the mixed emotions the Pilgrims must have had that day—the joy that half of their group had survived, and the sadness that half of their group had died.

On the familiar route from the apartment to my house, I thought about how I would explain Thanksgiving to someone if they asked me after tonight.

I decided I would show them the joy of new hats and gloves, a ride in my car, plates of turkey and stuffing eaten by Somali refugee children on a blanket in my living room, and an apartment filled with new clothes and enough supplies to get an African family through a Pacific Northwest winter. And I would show them the sadness of a little girl holding a tattered shirt against her cheek, weeping at the memory of the one who wasn't there.

This, I would say. *Thanksgiving is this.*

CHAPTER FORTY-SEVEN

THE ONLY GOOD thing about losing Ian, I told myself in the days after we broke up, was that at least I had now officially lost everything. I had touched bottom, and from here on out, I could only go up. It was a small consolation, but consoling nonetheless. And I needed some consolation as round after round after round of chemo took its toll on my weary body.

My oncologist had decided to give me dose-dense chemo, which meant I got an infusion every two weeks instead of every three. It also meant my body didn't have enough time to recover in between treatments, and the side effects accumulated quickly. It was like I was in a boxing match, competing with someone who was twice my weight. I kept getting knocked out, then staggering back into the ring for another round. But with every round, I grew more fragile and more despondent.

For the two weeks in between treatments, I would lie in bed feeling anxious. My brain, which was always going a million miles a minute, was trapped in a body that couldn't get out of bed. My joints ached as though I had a bad case of the flu. The hair follicles on my scalp ached. My mouth tasted like I was always sucking on a copper penny. My esophagus was inflamed, and felt like it was on fire every time I tried to eat or drink anything, which was difficult to begin with given the nausea and vomiting.

I tried everything I could think of to help mitigate the side effects. I took pain medicine. I wore soft caps on my head. I sucked on cough drops or lemon candies to get the foul taste out of my mouth. I took my nausea medicine religiously. I watched TV and played Scrabble with my mom to try to pass the time. And every day I made myself go outside, even if it was just to walk around the block once before getting back in bed.

One afternoon while I was getting a chemo infusion, the oncology social worker came to talk to me. She asked how I was doing, and I just shook my head while my eyes brimmed with tears. I had only been in treatment for one month, and I had six more to go. It felt like an eternity, and I had no idea how I was going to survive it.

"It's just *so long*," I said.

She told me to take it one day at a time, patted my hand, and left. I closed my eyes and turned my iPod to one of my new favorite songs, Judy Garland's version of "Somewhere Over the Rainbow."

One day at a time. A whole twenty-four hours of pain, vomiting, loneliness, and fear. Even a day felt like forever sometimes. I finally reduced my coping strategy to the very smallest increment. One breath. Just take this process one breath at a time, I told myself. If you can keep taking just one more breath, you'll get through this.

I thought I'd lost everything when Ian walked away, but then my disability claim got denied because, since I'd had cancer the year before, my recurrence was considered a preexisting condition. So I was facing seven months without any income. And then my car's air conditioner broke and I had to pay hundreds of dollars to get it fixed, because I couldn't imagine driving to and from chemo in 100-degree

July heat without it. And then, a few days after I paid to have my car fixed, it was hit by a moving truck in the parking lot of my apartment building.

Okay, now *I've lost everything,* I told myself as I surveyed my damaged car. *It definitely gets better from here.*

And then, after my third round of chemo, I found a dime-sized lump near my right mastectomy scar. I had yet another surgical consult, and then another biopsy. Two days later, my dad flew into town to visit for a long weekend. He and my mom and I were getting ready to walk to a café for lunch when my phone rang.

It was the surgeon. "The biopsy's back. It's cancer."

My body was growing more cancer even while I was on chemo. And they hadn't gotten it all during the biopsy, so I'd need yet another surgery to remove all of the cancer.

When I hung up the phone, I didn't have to tell my parents what the biopsy result was. They could see the desperation in my face.

"It's okay to cry," my dad said.

"I don't want to cry!" I yelled at him. And in defiance of my diagnosis, I didn't cry while we walked the five blocks to the café. I didn't cry while my parents stood in line to place our order, or while I found an empty table and saved our seats.

When they returned with a tray of chicken salad sandwiches and iced tea, my dad looked at me and said again, "It's okay to cry."

And even as I insisted again that I didn't *want* to cry, the tears were streaming down my face.

CHAPTER FORTY-EIGHT

B ECAUSE MY CANCER recurred so quickly and so aggressively, my oncologist decided I should undergo radiation before finishing chemo.

Every weekday for six weeks, my mom and I drove to the radiation oncology clinic. After I checked in, my mom sat in the waiting room while a nurse took me down the hall to a separate, patient-only waiting room that featured two changing rooms and an area with a few chairs, magazines, and a TV mounted on the wall.

Another nurse met me in this waiting room and, once I had changed into a gown, walked me down another hallway to a treatment room. I climbed up onto a narrow table and lay on my back with my arms outstretched.

Like Jesus on the cross, I thought.

The nurse pulled down a machine close to my chest, and lined up the red laser beam with markings on my torso. The radiation field included everything on the right side of my sternum, from my collarbone to halfway down my ribs. After everything was lined up, she left the room and turned on the machine. I lay there for about ten minutes by myself in a silent, cold room, pleading with God to let the treatment work. And every day as I pleaded with Him to spare my life, my eyes brimmed with tears that I could not brush away, because my arms were tethered down.

Like Jesus on the cross.

I didn't realize until later that there was a video camera on the wall, and the nurses could see me on the closed circuit screen in the control room. One of them said to me, "Your face looks so intense during your treatment. What are you thinking about?"

"I'm praying that my cancer goes away and never comes back," I said.

Every day for thirty days, I followed the same routine. I walked down the long hallway, got undressed from the waist up, put on a gown, and sat in the patient waiting room until one of the techs called me back to the treatment room.

It was in this waiting room that I met Dan, a sixty-something-year-old man with pancreatic cancer.

He used to be the CEO of a company in Tennessee, but he retired a few years before and started teaching economics at a local community college. Every time I saw him, he was in a hospital gown, but he still had a very dignified presence. He was tall, trim, and each of his gray hairs was always perfectly in place.

The housing market crashed that summer, and the stock market followed. Dan and I were both interested in the latest developments, so whoever got to the waiting room first would change the TV channel from daytime soap operas to CNBC, and together we would watch the business reports.

Sometimes we talked about stocks; other times we swapped stories about our lives. He told me about his job, his students, his wife and children and grandchildren. And I told him about my family and my journalism program, which I'd postponed until I finished treatments.

When I was driving to my final radiation session, Joan Osborne's song "One of Us" came on the radio. In the song, Osborne wonders about what conversations we'd have with God if He was one of us. *What would you ask if you had just one question?* she sings.

I thought about the lyrics as I parked my dented car. If I could ask God just one question, what would it be?

It didn't take me long to decide my answer. I would ask Him, *Why?*

When I checked in for my last treatment, I hugged the nurses who had taken care of me for six weeks, and gave them a plant—because the radiation suite was in the basement and all their plants kept dying. And as a parting gift to me, the nurses gave me a box of Kleenex, because they had never seen a patient cry so much.

As I sat with Dan in the patient waiting room for the last time, I was still thinking about Joan Osborne's lyrics.

"If you got to ask God one question, what would you ask Him?" I asked Dan.

He thought about it for a minute, then answered, "I don't know."

I thought about how desperate I was to know why. *Why me? Why this? Why now? Why again?* I wanted something in this nightmare to make sense.

I said, "Would you ask God why?"

He shook his head vehemently. "No, no, no."

"Why not?"

"Because..." he began. "Because I don't think there's a good 'why.' Because even if I did know why, what would it matter? What would it change?"

He turned back to the stock reports as I contemplated his answer. Of course he was right, but it didn't change my longing to have an explanation for my suffering.

CHAPTER FORTY-NINE

E VERY TIME I told people I had breast cancer, they would always cock their heads, furrow their brows, and say, "But you're
so *young...*"

And I would always nod politely to these well-intentioned
Masters of the Obvious, and try not to let on how badly I wanted
to be able to offer them (and me) a satisfactory explanation. But
there wasn't one. I hadn't smoked, hadn't drunk, hadn't eaten lots of
red meat, hadn't been overweight, hadn't taken birth control pills. I
hadn't even used antiperspirant deodorant because I'd read in college
that it might cause breast cancer.

The only explanation my oncologist could think of when I was
first diagnosed was maybe I had the BRCA gene that predisposes
women to breast and ovarian cancer. So he sent me to the Yale
Cancer Center Genetic Counseling Department for a BRCA blood
test after my mastectomy. A few weeks later, I returned to the center
with two friends to receive my results. The genetic counselor came
in, slid a paper across the table, and said aloud what I was reading on
the report in front of me: "Negative for the BRCA gene."

A few moments later, standing on the sidewalk in front of the building, my friends congratulated me and hugged me. "That's such good news!" they exclaimed, then hurried back to work. I stood there on the sidewalk long after they'd walked away. It *was* good news, but it didn't make me feel any better; it made me feel even more like a sitting duck. If no one knew why I got the cancer, how could I prevent it from coming back?

And then it *had* recurred, a year after my mastectomy. And every day of treatment, through seven months of chemo and radiation, I wondered why. And then I started to wonder if Dan wasn't right. Knowing why wouldn't matter. It wouldn't change or fix anything. Besides, I concluded, maybe I was better off not knowing why than receiving an answer from God.

Since I was little, the voice of God in my head had been punishing and severe. I had spent most of my adult life trying to change that voice, trying to believe that God was more loving than the vindictive patriarch I'd constructed from the Sunday school stories of judgment and hell. At least in the absence of answers, I could assume the best about Him.

Part of me was afraid that if I raised my fist to the sky and demanded an answer now, I would hear a thundering and calloused, "Because I said so," from God in heaven.

And I may not ever want to speak to Him again.

CHAPTER FIFTY

THE DOCTOR AT THE free clinic diagnosed Chaki with an ear infection and gave Hadhi bottles of Children's Tylenol and amoxicillin. When we got home, I showed Hadhi how to measure out the doses of the medicines, and explained when to give them. She watched as I measured the first dose of the antibiotic and gave it to Chaki.

Chaki swallowed a teaspoon of the thick pink liquid, but as soon as she got it down, she started running around the apartment, wiping her mouth on anything she could find. "It's NO GOOD! It's NO GOOD! I NO LIKE your medicine!" she yelled.

When Fahari, Abdallah, and Sadaka got home from school that day, I left to pick up two pizzas. While we ate together on the dining room floor that evening, the girls started telling me how discouraged they were with school. They were tired of being mocked because their clothes were dirty and didn't fit well. They didn't have any treats to share with their classmates at lunch like the other kids did. They didn't have any pens or pencils to do their homework with.

While we were eating, Lelo broke into the fridge to try to get more juice. She couldn't reach the top shelf, so she stood on the bottom rack on the refrigerator door, and it snapped in two. Lelo and the rack and a gallon of SunnyD juice fell to the floor. Hadhi ran into the kitchen to see what the loud crash was from. She returned with the broken rack, scolding a tearful Lelo.

"Look, Sarah, look!" Hadhi said, dropping the two pieces into my lap.

She started speaking rapid Somali, and Fahari translated. "My mom's afraid that if the apartment manager sees this, he'll kick us out. And then he'll send us back to Somalia."

I shook my head. "Definitely not," I said. "I'll buy some glue and we'll fix the door. It'll be okay."

After dinner, Hadhi pulled the week's unopened mail out of her purse and asked me to open it and read it to them. There was a letter from the school threatening that if they didn't receive the girls' immunization records that week, they'd be kicked out of school. Their first winter electric bill was due—and it was over a hundred dollars.

Hadhi reached her breaking point before we could open all the mail. She dropped down into a chair in the living room and held her head in her hands. "It's broken," she said. "Everything in America is broken."

Fahari sat down at her feet and tried to put a reassuring hand on her mom's knee. Hadhi brushed it away. "No. No. No. America is broken."

My heart broke for Hadhi—for all of them. For how far they'd had to come, and for how far they still had to go. I reminded Hadhi that I had friends who cared about them and wanted to help them, and we were working on raising money to help with the electric bill so they could keep their heat on. I told her that my church had started a kids' clothing drive, so the girls would soon have clean, well-fitting outfits. Then I reached into my purse and pulled out pens for the girls to use to complete their homework.

I pointed to all of these things as evidence that we were going to get through these rough waters. We might be a little dinghy that was getting pummeled by forceful gales, but I was confident that we would get through the storm without breaking.

After the girls finished their homework, I gave them some chocolates and asked Hadhi to play the cassette tape of African music she had brought from Somalia. She had used some of the spare change they'd collected to buy an old cassette tape player at Goodwill. She retrieved it from her bedroom, then plugged it into an outlet and hit play.

She disappeared into her bedroom again, and emerged with an African dress, a headscarf, and large bangle bracelets for me. When she and the girls had dressed me up in my new Somali outfit, we formed a line and I led them on a dancing procession through the living room, into the kitchen, down the hall, and back to the living room. When the song was over, we collapsed into a pile on the floor, giggling until our cheeks hurt from smiling so much.

After all the girls had fallen asleep that night, I sat with Hadhi in the hallway outside the girls' room, drinking coffee and talking about Somalia. She seemed to be feeling more optimistic about her situation. She told me that when she got her green card, she wanted to take me back to visit her father and siblings, who still lived in Africa.

And then in broken English she said, "I will tell them about America. I will tell them America is broken." She sighed, and dropped her weary, brown-eyed gaze to the floor. She was quiet for a few minutes as she considered everything her family had been through in the past year, and all the hurdles that were to come.

She reached for my hand. "But God gave us Sahara," she said, offering a weak smile. "So everything will be okay…" But from the silent pleading in her eyes, I could tell it was more of a question than a statement.

I wrapped my hands around hers and echoed, "Everything will be okay."

CHAPTER FIFTY-ONE

THE NEXT TIME I went over to the apartment, Sadaka ran to the door holding a cup filled with dry Cheerios. "The milk fell down! The milk fell down!" she cried. "You mean it spilled?" I asked.

"No, it fell down," she insisted.

I asked her to show me what she meant, so she took my hand and led me into the kitchen and opened the fridge door. I saw four gallons of milk that Hadhi had gotten from the WIC program. Sadaka pulled the nearest one out, unscrewed the lid, and began to pour it into an empty cup. It looked more like cottage cheese than milk, and it smelled sour.

"Sweetheart, it's spoiled," I said.

She nodded vigorously. "It fell down. *All* the milk fell down." She pointed to the other containers of milk, most of which had spoiled as well.

Hadhi came into the kitchen and explained, with Sadaka translating, that they'd never had cow's milk in Africa, and they didn't know what to do with it.

I realized as I was talking to her that she also didn't know how a refrigerator worked. The little girls would open the door to get some fruit or juice out, and they'd leave the door open. Hadhi didn't realize that in order for the fridge to stay cold, the door had to be closed.

She asked me how to tell if milk was good or bad. I put the gallons side by side on the counter and showed her the expiration dates and explained that if it was more than seven days after the expiration date, it was bad.

But she wasn't used to keeping track of time with dates and numbers. Every time I left their apartment, I would tell her when I was coming back, so she knew that I wasn't leaving forever. I would hold up my fingers and say, "I'll be back in three days. One, two, three," as I counted out the days on my fingers. But it never stuck. She would call me every day, asking where I was and when I was coming back.

Since expiration dates didn't make sense to her, I took the caps off all the gallons and told her she could also smell the milk to see if it had gone bad.

"If you don't smell anything, it's good milk," I said. "If it smells bad, it's spoiled, and you should throw it away."

There was one unspoiled gallon, so I made Hadhi and the three older girls smell that one first. Then I passed around the spoiled gallons. They scrunched their noses and stuck out their tongues. "Exactly," I said. "Smelly milk is no good," and then I made an exaggerated demonstration of how to pour it down the drain.

Later that afternoon, after the milk and other spoiled food had been disposed of, Hadhi invited me to have lunch with them. She brought out a deep dish of rice and boiled potatoes covered with meat and curry sauce.

We all sat around on the floor, dipped our right hands in a bowl of clean water, then began eating the food. It was delicious, but I couldn't place the meat. It tasted a little bit like beef, but it was chewier—like pork.

"What's the Somali word for this?" I asked Sadaka, holding up a piece. She told me the Somali word for meat.

"No, I mean, what *kind* of meat? What animal does it come from?" I asked.

"Oh," she said casually. "That's goat."

CHAPTER FIFTY-TWO

WHILE WE ATE curried goat for dinner, the girls told me they had big news to share. "Fahari started bleeding!" they all announced simultaneously when I asked them what was new. And that's how I found out that nine-year-old Fahari had started her period.

The girls had lots of questions about what was happening, and what it meant, and what you were supposed to do about it. I don't have kids, so I didn't have an official Facts of Life talk prepared. But I did have a master's degree in medical science and some experience working in women's health, so I decided I was as qualified as anyone to answer their questions.

We cleared the dinner dishes and washed the curry off our hands, and then we all sat in a circle in the living room. Hadhi sat with us, too, eager to learn about the science behind the phenomenon, and how women in America handle menstruation.

I started by asking them if they knew what female anatomy was called. Sadaka, the six-year-old, shouted, "It's called your *ass*," and she giggled.

"Nope," I said.

She looked hurt and said, more subdued, "Well, that's what the kids at school call it."

"*Ass* is another word for your bottom," I said. "We're talking about a different part."

And with that introduction, we were off. With big, vague brush-strokes—trying only to include what little girls needed to know—I explained the particulars of human sexuality. After a few minutes of conversation, with anatomy explained and questions answered, the girls lost interest and ran off to play.

Hadhi and I sat alone in the living room.

"Are you sure she's only nine?" I asked. Since I met Fahari, I was suspicious that, given her height and curves, she may be older than her stated age. Now that she'd started her period, I was almost certain of it.

Hadhi explained in broken English that when they emigrated from Somalia, they didn't have birth certificates, so U.S. government employees had estimated the girls' ages. Hadhi told me that African children are smaller than American children because their nutrition isn't as good, so often the African children appear younger than they really are.

"How old is Fahari? Do you know?" I asked.

She shook her head.

"Do you remember what year she was born?"

Hadhi again shook her head.

I tried to do the math a different way. "Do you remember how old you were when you had her?" I asked.

She shook her head again.

Suddenly I had a new appreciation for Fahari's struggles in America. She was supposedly a nine-year-old, who was in a first-grade classroom, who had just started her period. I couldn't imagine how disorienting it was not to know how old you were, or where you really belonged in society.

While I was thinking about this, Hadhi got up and brought me another stack of unopened mail. There was a lot of junk mail, and a few more bills. When I opened the phone bill, I saw it was two months overdue, and they were threatening to close the account if it wasn't paid.

"Your phone bill's overdue," I explained to Hadhi.

She shrugged. "No money," she said.

I thought about what it would mean for Hadhi not to have this link to the outside world. What if she needed to call for help? What if she or the girls needed to get ahold of me? I thought about paying it just this once, but then I realized it wouldn't be a one-time expense, and if I started paying her bills for her, Hadhi would never gain her independence.

As I handed the bill back to her, Hadhi looked at me expectantly, as if to ask me what we were going to do about it.

"If you can't pay the bill, they'll turn your phone off," I said. "I'm really sorry."

When I'd spoken to people about the Somali family, many of them referenced the famous quote, "If you give a man a fish, you'll feed him for a day. If you teach him to fish, you'll feed him for life." But as I was considering Hadhi's situation, I wondered, *How can you teach a man to fish if he doesn't even know where the water is?*

I drove home that night feeling uncertain and, once again, overwhelmed. I wanted to be the one who got to share good things with the family—like the money, furniture, food, and the clothes my friends and church family had donated. Discussing details of womanhood and overdue utility bills was not something I particularly enjoyed, and it made me feel even more inadequate than usual.

CHAPTER FIFTY-THREE

I NEVER HEARD my parents say the word *sex* until I was almost finished with high school. The reality of sex was shrouded in euphemisms and hyperreligious lingo.

Thanks to my curious and scientifically oriented mind, I figured out sex for myself when I was thirteen years old. I had been babysitting two children for the summer, and I noted the difference in female and male anatomy when I changed their diapers. I noticed that boys had round pegs, and girls had round holes. It seemed to me that if all men had pegs and all women had holes, these were most likely puzzle pieces that were meant to fit together. And then I thought I must be crazy, because how could you *ever* let a boy's peg anywhere near your hole?

My curiosity finally overcame my embarrassment, and I decided to research my theory. One evening, while my parents were out and my younger siblings were asleep, I took the *R* encyclopedia off the bookcase in the living room and retreated to my room.

Looking back, I realize I should have taken the *S* encyclopedia to look up *Sex*, but at the time, I didn't even know what it was called. The only word I knew that pertained to the topic was *Re-*

production, which I must have picked up in biology class at some point.

I sat on the floor of my bedroom with knees tucked to my chest, serving as a makeshift tabletop for the encyclopedia that lay open in front of me. With alternating exclamations of "Wow!" and "Ewww!" I read the chapter from start to finish.

The following year, when I was attending middle school at a small Christian school in rural New Jersey, I discovered not just what sex was, but what it did to women. I stayed after class one afternoon to get some extra math tutoring from my teacher. But instead of helping me with my algebra homework, he took a stack of photos from the top drawer of his desk.

He pushed my math textbook and notebook paper to the edge of the desk, and began to flip through photographs of his wife, who had just had a baby a few weeks before. In the first pictures she was wearing a hospital gown and lying in a hospital bed, grimacing with contractions. Then she was sweaty and tearful. Then she was lying on her back with her feet in stirrups, naked from the waist down, and a baby's head was emerging from her vagina.

"*This* is what women were made for," my teacher told me.

I was too shocked by the graphic images to say anything, too embarrassed to move. As I sat there in my chair uncertain of what to do next, wishing to disappear, I felt deeply ashamed. Not just because I was sitting alone in a classroom with a male teacher looking at pictures of his wife's genitals, but also because I had dared to take science and math classes when the other girls were sewing aprons in the home ec room down the hall. Why was I asking a man for help with algebra when I was clearly designed for another fate?

I thought of the geometry theorem this man had taught me the year before, that a whole is equal to the sum of its parts. I was two breasts, two ovaries, one uterus, and one vagina, which equaled one reproducing female. Nothing more.

I didn't ask him for help after that. Instead I spent two or three hours a night in my room, teaching math to myself. *I'm more than the sum of my reproductive organs,* I thought. *I also have a brain.*

When I moved on to precalculus, my parents didn't have the $100 needed to buy me a graphing calculator. So instead I bought a ream of graphing paper from the dollar store and painstakingly plotted all the equations by hand. I worked multiple odd jobs to earn my way through college. Getting into Yale was confirmation of what I'd been telling myself for a decade. *I also have a brain.*

One afternoon I was walking through the atrium of the hospital, on my way to spend the afternoon in the clinic, when a tall man in a long white lab coat stopped me.

"Excuse me, do you have a minute?" he asked. He introduced himself as an OB/GYN. We sat down on a bench near the fountain in the center of the lobby, and he explained he was working with a couple in the fertility clinic, and he was wondering if I would be willing to donate my eggs.

"You're just what they're looking for," he said. "A thin, pretty, blond Yale grad student. They'd pay you twenty thousand dollars."

I was speechless. He put his business card in the palm of my hand, then stood up to leave.

"Think about it," he said. "The most you'd get from the other fertility clinics is eight grand."

As he walked away, I thought, *I also have a brain.* Although the amount of money he was offering was almost as much as the scholarship Yale had given me, so maybe my reproductive organs were the sum of me after all.

CHAPTER FIFTY-FOUR

T HE SOMALI GIRLS hadn't even lived in the United States for a year before they became obsessed with the Disney princesses. They asked if I could get them gowns and wands and tiaras, because they thought that if they wore these costumes to school, the other kids would see how important and special they were.

Hadhi, on the other hand, was not into princesses or romance at all. I often went over to find her watching *Jerry Springer*. She didn't understand what they were saying, but she could tell what the show was about when she saw two jealous women and one sheepish man sitting together on the stage. And she lived for the moment they started throwing chairs.

"They fighting! Everybody fighting!" she would say as she laughed.

"Fighting is no good, Hadhi," I said, trying to get her to change the channel. "We don't like fighting. It's no good."

"No good," she'd repeat as she laughed and kept watching the show.

One evening I went over to the apartment with a pizza, which we ate together on the living room floor while Hadhi tried to find a movie for us to watch on TV. She settled on a movie I'd never seen. It was fine until the scene when, while at a dinner party, a couple starts arguing. They get up and leave the table, and start arguing in the foyer of the home. While they argue, they start hitting each other, and the man starts punching the woman. And then he grabs her hair and drags her across the floor.

I was appalled. "Hadhi, no! The girls cannot watch this. Change the channel."

Hadhi pointed to the TV and said, "That's my husband."

As the man slapped and punched and kicked the woman on the screen, I realized that this story resonated with Hadhi because it had happened to her. And by pointing to the screen, she was able to show me in images what her limited English wouldn't allow her to say.

My heart broke for her. But still. We were sitting there with five little impressionable girls watching the horrific scene unfold.

"Hadhi, change it to cartoons. This is no good," I said again.

She didn't change the channel. She kept saying, "My husband, my husband."

I didn't want to undermine her authority in the home by getting up and changing the channel myself, but it was also unconscionable to stay while the girls watched these images. God forbid they would ever come to think it was normal for men to treat women this way.

The only other option I could think of was to leave. "Hadhi," I said, standing up. "This movie is very bad. If you don't change it to cartoons, I have to go home."

Finally, she switched it to *SpongeBob SquarePants*, and I sat back down. As the girls giggled at the cartoon, I studied their beautiful skin and warm smiles, and remembered how I felt when I was their age. For all the differences between evangelical Christian and fundamental Muslim religions, the culture these extreme groups created for women was very similar.

I knew from experience what it was like to be shrouded under yards of ill-fitting fabric. To fear your sexuality—sometimes even the parts of you that you never knew could be sexual, like your elbows and ankles and shoulders and knees. To live with the assumption that you are not complete and cannot fulfill your purpose in life without a man to impregnate and provide for you.

I wondered how I could help these girls grow up to be women who were too confident to wait for a man to rescue them, and too valuable to stay with a man who abused them. Teaching them these values seemed like an ambitious goal, especially given their more pressing needs.

I was becoming overwhelmed at just the thought of all of the problems they were facing. There was no way I could help solve them all at once. I thought of something my dean told me when I was overwhelmed in grad school, and didn't see how I could do clinical rotations, attend class, take exams, and write a thesis at the same time.

"How do you eat an elephant?" she asked.

I shook my head, too exhausted to unravel her riddle.

"One bite at a time," she said.

One bite at a time.

CHAPTER FIFTY-FIVE

THE FIRST STEP in helping the Somali girls adjust to life in America was to ensure they had their basic needs of shelter, clothing, and food met. The next step was to try to teach them living skills—how to turn on the heat, how to use the oven, how to wash their hands with soap, and how to use toilet paper.

After that, I focused on showing Hadhi how to take care of the things they had. I showed her how to keep the food they had from spoiling, how to wash the clothes they'd been given, how to take care of their new furniture.

The next step was to teach the essential social skills—how to share, how to express feelings and opinions, and how to resolve conflict without resorting to physical violence.

Karina lived close to me. Since she was a stay-at-home mom, I asked her to work with Hadhi to teach her household logistics like how to budget, pay bills, grocery shop, and keep track of time.

I bought Hadhi a calculator to keep track of how much she was spending on food and utilities. One afternoon just before Christmas, Karina and I went over to the apartment. While I played with the kids, Karina sat with Hadhi and Fahari and taught them how to add and subtract using the calculator, how to tell time using a watch, and how to track a schedule using the calendar.

After that tutorial, Hadhi became very interested in numbers. She started asking me to tell her the date, and she repeated the number a few times until she was confident she could remember it. When I called her on the phone to tell her I was coming over that day, she'd ask me what time I was coming. And when I brought something over to the apartment, she asked me how much it cost.

How much is a pair of socks? How much is a box of crayons? How much is a pound of grapes?

When I drove Hadhi and the two girls to Chaki's doctor appointment, Hadhi announced that she needed a car so she could take her family around town without having to wait for the bus.

"How much your car?" she asked.

I froze for a second. Should I tell her how much I'd paid for my car? Would it increase the distance between us if she realized how different my lifestyle was compared to hers? I decided in the end that I should be honest with her. If she was going to thrive in America, and teach her girls how to succeed as well, she needed to have a realistic understanding of the economy they were living in.

"My car cost nine thousand dollars," I told her honestly.

She pulled out her wallet and began to count one-dollar bills and some spare change, thinking I'd said it cost me nine dollars.

I shook my head. "No, nine thousand," I said.

"Nine hundred?" she asked.

"No. Thousand. Nine thousand."

Her eyes grew wide. "So much money for a little car?" she asked.

I nodded, and then smiled. "Cars are very expensive," I said. "So the bus is very good for now."

She nodded. "Yah, the bus very good," she said.

CHAPTER FIFTY-SIX

H ADHI'S SICK," Karina told me when she called me one afternoon. I'd worked several shifts in a row at the clinic and hadn't had the time to check on the family, so Karina had offered to go instead. She said Hadhi had paperwork from her doctor's office, and from what she could tell, they were doing a workup for malaria.

The next night I went over to the apartment to check on everyone. On my way I stopped to pick up sandwiches, pretzels, and fruit for dinner. When I walked in the door, I found Hadhi lying on a mattress in the living room, buried under a pile of covers. The five little girls were sitting around her bed, as quiet as I'd ever seen them.

Abdallah looked up as I walked in, and with tears in her eyes told me, "Mommy's sick."

I walked over to Hadhi and pulled the blankets back so I could take a look at her. She moaned and fluttered her eyes, then closed them again. I felt her forehead with the back of my hand.

"You have a fever," I said.

"Yah, fever. Malaria," she said.

I pulled a bottle of Tylenol out of my bag and gave her two tablets and some water. She sat up to take the medicine, then lay down again. I set dinner out for the girls, and we sat in a circle on the floor and ate together, talking softly so Hadhi could try to sleep.

But before we finished eating, Hadhi was crying, holding her head. I walked back over to her bed. "Hadhi, do you need to go to the hospital?" I asked her.

"Yah," she said. "Hospital. Emergency."

I said a quick prayer that she wouldn't die of sepsis or meningitis or malaria before I could get her there—and then took action.

I called my housemates to come stay with the girls. While we were waiting for them to come, I cleaned up dinner and asked Fahari to sweep the floor. I got Hadhi's coat and shoes and helped her put them on. As soon as she was dressed, she went back under the covers, complaining she was cold even though she was burning up with a fever.

When Betsy and Karrie arrived, we did a quick trade-off. I explained a little bit about the girls and the apartment, then got Hadhi settled in the passenger seat of my car and drove her to the hospital.

We checked in at the front desk of the ER, then sat down and waited for the triage nurse to call us. While we were sitting there in uncomfortable, vinyl-covered chairs under blazing fluorescent lights, Hadhi leaned forward and buried her face in her hands.

"It's too much," she said, sobbing. "Fever, malaria, five girls. My dad in Somalia, my mom dead. No sisters in America. No money. It's too much."

I had rarely seen Hadhi cry, so her tears broke my heart. I put my arms around her. "We'll get you medicine to help you feel better," I told her. "It will be okay. God loves you, and Karina and I will be your sisters in America, okay?"

She nodded and brushed the tears from her eyes, then slept with her head on my shoulder until the triage nurse called her name.

CHAPTER FIFTY-SEVEN

AN HOUR AFTER we arrived at the ER, Hadhi was triaged and assigned to a room in the back of the ER. The nurse set out a gown on the gurney, and asked her to get undressed and get into bed. I offered to leave to let Hadhi preserve her privacy, but she was so sick, she was unconcerned about modesty.

"Help," she whimpered as she made an unsuccessful attempt to undress herself.

I helped her untie her shoes, take off her jacket, and remove her clothes. I helped her into the clean hospital gown, then tucked her in between the crisp white sheets. She sighed and closed her eyes as her head sank against the plush pillow beneath her head. I wondered when was the last time she'd been able to climb into bed and close her eyes without having to worry about the locks on the front door or her five children in the next room.

I tucked the sheet under her chin, leaned down, and kissed her forehead. "It's going to be okay," I whispered.

With her eyes closed, she nodded—though I could still see the tearstains on her cheeks. I picked up the call light next to her bed. "Look, you can even watch TV for free!"

We settled on the nature channel, and watched it until her doctor entered the room. When he came in, I introduced myself and explained a little bit about Hadhi's symptoms and what she'd been through the past week.

"How do you know her?" he asked.

"I met her on the MAX," I said.

"Tonight?" he asked.

"No, about four months ago. I met her and her girls on the MAX and I've been trying to help them get adjusted to life in the States."

He nodded with vague uncertainty, as if he lacked a category for this answer.

He got a Somali interpreter on the phone to ask Hadhi more about her symptoms. The Somali interpreter said, "Hi, my name is Lelo. How can I help you?"

With the woman on the other end of the line translating, Hadhi explained how she was feeling, and the doctor told her what tests he was going to order. He also said that in the meantime, they'd give Hadhi an IV with some fluids and pain medication since she had such a bad headache and was also complaining of abdominal pain.

After the doctor left the room, Hadhi lay back in bed, closed her eyes, and smiled. "Lelo," she said.

I'd thought the same thing. The interpreter's name was the same as her fourth child's. I imagined the four-year-old Lelo I knew as a woman, fluent in English and Somali, working as a medical interpreter. And for a few minutes in the overcrowded ER, Hadhi and I saw a glimmer of hope as we imagined a future for her girls.

CHAPTER FIFTY-EIGHT

Hadhi's doctor came back to the room a few hours later. Her X-rays and labs were normal. There were no signs of malaria or a bacterial infection; she probably just had a bad virus, he said. He gave her prescriptions for pain and nausea medicine, and then discharged her.

We drove to the pharmacy and handed in her prescriptions. Hadhi had perked up considerably after several liters of IV fluids. Since we had time to kill while we waited for her medicines, I asked her if she was hungry. She nodded vigorously, and I wondered how many days it had been since she'd felt well enough to eat.

We walked to the refrigerated section, where there were pre-made sandwiches and soft drinks. She picked up a bottle of Coke and smiled. "Coca-Cola," she said, winking at me.

Then she studied the sandwiches, picking them up one by one and examining their contents under the bright overhead fluorescent light. Finally she gave up and shrugged. "They pork?" she asked.

I'd forgotten both about her Muslim dietary guidelines, and the fact that she couldn't read. She couldn't tell which sandwiches had pig products and which ones were safe. I picked up a roast beef and cheese sandwich. "Beef," I said.

She nodded. "Beef good," she said.

We walked up front to the cash register and paid for her food, then sat in chairs by the pharmacy while she ate. In less than five minutes she had consumed half of the sandwich, and half of the Coke. I could tell she was still hungry, but she wrapped up the other half of the sandwich and gave it to me to put in my purse. "Fahari, Abdallah, Sadaka, Lelo, Chaki…" she said, and I understood that she was saving the other half of the sandwich for her girls.

When she leaned her head on my shoulder again and closed her eyes, I saw Hadhi in a new light. I had spent months helping her take care of her five girls, ensuring that the girls had a chance at a good education and plenty of food and clean clothes and toys. But maybe in focusing on the children, I had overlooked Hadhi, who in many ways was still a girl herself.

She had experienced three children's deaths, her mother's death, genocide, starvation, and abuse. But in spite of the wisdom she'd gained from all her life experiences, she was lost in this new culture and didn't have the tools she needed to function. She didn't have the right kind of education or experience to teach her girls how to live in this new place. Since she couldn't read, she didn't know the difference between the words *broil* and *on* on the stove dials. She didn't understand how to turn on the heat. She couldn't even pick out a sandwich by herself.

She was caught between impassable paradoxes: The same regime that made its followers abide by strict dietary laws had also denied Hadhi the right to attend school long enough to be able to read the labels on food containers. The culture that made her marry as a teenager and become completely dependent on her husband also gave him the autonomy to abuse Hadhi, lock her and the girls in an apartment without any provisions, and then run away, leaving them desolate.

I realized she was as trapped as anyone by her culture and circumstances, but because she was responsible for her daughters' welfare, it was easy for me to overlook her on the way to assessing what her girls needed.

As I felt the weight of Hadhi's sleeping form resting on me while we waited for the pharmacist to fill her prescriptions, I saw what I had missed before.

Hadhi was an Invisible Girl, too.

CHAPTER FIFTY-NINE

WHEN MY RADIATION treatments finished, I had four more rounds of chemo. Two days after my last infusion, I started coughing. I made an appointment at the cancer center, and the nurse practitioner examined me. "Let's get a chest X-ray," she said at the end of the visit.

Later that afternoon she called to tell me I had a small area of pneumonia on the X-ray. She phoned in an antibiotic to the pharmacy.

The following night, I was lying on the couch watching TV when I realized my heart was racing. I checked my pulse, and instead of being in the normal range of 60–100, it was beating 180 times a minute. I phoned the on-call oncologist. He answered with a yawn, and I realized it was close to midnight.

When I told him my heart was racing and I was having a difficult time breathing, he said, "You either have a blood clot in your lung, or your pneumonia's getting worse. I'll meet you at the ER in twenty minutes."

It had been four months since Ian had left me and I hadn't talked to him once, but now, as I was ill and possibly dying, he was the only person I could think to call. Fifteen minutes after I called him, he pulled up to my apartment in his car. I climbed in wearing pajama pants and an oversized Yale sweatshirt, with a backpack filled with clothes, books, and my laptop.

"Hey, kid," he said as I was fastening my seat belt. "How've you been?"

"Awesome," I said as I leaned my bald head against the window and fought to breathe. A few minutes later, we pulled up to the ER entrance. Ian kept the car running as I picked up my backpack and opened my door.

"Are you coming in?" I asked.

He shook his head. "Good luck," he said, "I'll call you later." And he drove away.

Once I was triaged and assigned a bed, I got a chest X-ray, labs, and several liters of IV fluids. When I got back from getting the X-ray, I started having a harder time breathing, and felt like there was a crushing load of bricks on my chest. My nurse gave me a shot of morphine for the pain.

"I'm dying, aren't I?" I asked her as she threw the needle into the red plastic bin hanging on the wall. She hurried out of the room without saying anything.

An hour later, the head physician came into my room and sat down on the edge of my bed. "Your entire right lung is filled with fluid and infection," he said. "It's a complete white-out on the chest X-ray. Your white count is triple what it should be, and you're severely anemic. You've had liters of fluids and your pulse isn't coming down, and your blood pressure isn't going up."

"What does all that mean?" I asked, too tired to process the clinical data he was giving me.

"You're in sepsis," he said. "I'm sending you to the ICU as soon as there's a bed available."

An hour after that, I went unconscious and my breathing slowed to five respirations a minute. I woke up to a doctor forcing air into my lungs with an Ambu bag, debating with a doctor standing on the other side of me who was going to intubate me. I knew that many patients who went on a ventilator never come off it, so I fought to stay awake. With all the energy I had, I pulled air into my lungs, and then forced it out. Every breath was an exhausting effort.

Since my miserable chemo treatments a few months before, I'd told myself I could survive this ordeal by taking it one breath at a time. Now I wondered, *What happens when I run out of breath?*

The doctors didn't intubate me, but they did move me to the critical care section of the ER so they could resuscitate me if I started to die. There were still no beds in the ICU. After several hours of IV antibiotics and fluids and a blood transfusion, my pulse and blood pressure improved, and breathing became a little easier. At noon the next day, I was still in the ER. I had spent the last twelve hours there alone, and there were still no openings in the ICU.

That's when Rajah, my friend from church that I hadn't seen in months, showed up with his Bible and a cafeteria tray filled with chicken nuggets, french fries, and a Diet Coke. "It's the only food they had," he explained. "But I thought you might be hungry."

I thanked him, and then tried to eat some of the food he'd brought.

"How are you?" he asked.

I have no idea, I thought as I took a sip of Coke. After a few bites, I closed my eyes and drifted off to sleep, wondering if I was dying, wondering if Diet Coke and french fries were going to be my last supper.

Rajah opened his Bible, put his hand on my feverish forehead, leaned in close, and read in a hushed voice:

The LORD is my shepherd; I shall not want. He maketh me to lie down in green pastures: he leadeth me beside the still waters. He restoreth my soul: he leadeth me in the paths of righteousness for his name's sake. Yea, though I walk through the valley of the shadow of death, I will fear no evil: for thou art with me...(Psalm 23:1–4 KJV).

CHAPTER SIXTY

A s I DRIFTED IN and out of consciousness in the ER, I remembered meeting Rajah at church on a hot summer Sunday afternoon in New Haven two years before. We quickly became friends as we attended the same Bible study, hung out with the same friends, and sang together on the worship team.

I was single because I had a hectic grad school schedule; he was single because he was waiting for his family in India to arrange his marriage. We had long talks about relationships and dating and marriage, and both bemoaned the high divorce rate in the United States.

Rajah theorized that maybe if marriage vows weren't so sappy, couples might have a more realistic expectation of what they were committing to. We spent one summer afternoon lying side by side on our backs in the grass of the New Haven Green, composing our imaginary vows to our imaginary spouses.

"How 'bout this," I said. "I love you, but you drive me crazy sometimes. I want to marry you, but I know it's going to be a lot of hard work. I promise to encourage you to do your best, but also love you at your worst, if you promise to do the same for me. Sometimes life together is going to suck, but in the end, it'll be worth it."

I remembered Rajah throwing back his head and laughing. "Make sure you invite me to your wedding," he said. Shortly after that I'd met Ian, and Rajah and I had fallen out of touch. Now, as I felt his hand on my forehead and heard his soft voice reading through the Psalms, it seemed my funeral was much more likely than my wedding.

Rajah stayed with me for a few hours, until I was finally moved to the ICU. The first night I was in the unit, I couldn't sleep. My body was giving out, but my mind was fully alert, so I took my laptop out of my backpack and connected to the hospital's WiFi network. Once I was online, I googled *sepsis*.

As I read the medical literature, I learned that patients admitted to the ICU with sepsis had a 50-50 chance of ever leaving the hospital. I called my parents in Illinois. They knew about my pneumonia diagnosis two days before, but I hadn't told them about my ER visit because I didn't want to worry them, and because there wasn't anything they could do about my infection from a distance.

When my mom picked up the phone, I told her I'd been admitted to the ICU. I tried to paint an accurate picture of my health without divulging the daunting statistics.

"I think you'd better come," I told her as the number *50-50* echoed in my head. When I hung up the phone, I realized the real reason I wanted my parents here was not so they could keep me company while I was in the hospital, but so I could have the chance to say good-bye.

The bacterial infection that started in my lungs progressed in spite of five different IV antibiotics. I was weary from chemo and the infection, and my major organs were starting to shut down. My parents drove through the night from Illinois to Connecticut, and every day they held a vigil at my bedside. My dad left after a week because he had to get back to his job at the church, but my mom stayed with me.

Two weeks into my hospital stay, my younger brother Matthew was getting married in Indiana. I had to decide if I wanted to try to make the wedding or not. In spite of all the antibiotics, the infection in my lungs had barely improved, and I knew I was probably going to die. As I contemplated my decision, I figured I had two options: I could go to the wedding and die, or miss the wedding and still probably die. So I gambled on the former option, and made my oncologist discharge me from the hospital so I could make it to Indiana by the following day for the ceremony.

On the day I was to be discharged, I woke up feeling nauseated. As soon as I sat up, I threw up all over my breakfast tray. Then I started wheezing, and had to get respiratory therapy. And then my blood pressure dropped and I had to get more IV fluids. And then my nurse came in to do chest physiotherapy, which involved her beating on my back so hard I felt like my teeth were going to fall out of my head. After that, my pulmonologist came in and told me the pneumonia had gotten worse overnight, in spite of all the antibiotics I was on.

My oncologist came in a few minutes later and said, "Your white blood cell count spiked today, and you're very anemic. You really shouldn't leave the hospital."

"I don't care," I said. "Let me go."

I was too ill to fly, so my aunt and uncle drove up from Baltimore and picked my mom and me up from the hospital. I climbed in with my backpack, which was filled with clothes, my wig, and half a dozen bottles of antibiotics and cough medicine. My mom and aunt made me a bed in the backseat of the SUV, and I slept while my uncle drove fifteen hours through the night to get us to Indianapolis by the following morning.

I wasn't in the wedding party, so the only thing I had to do was stand up for family pictures after the ceremony. I managed to stay upright for the photos, and then I walked to the buffet line in the church fellowship hall, where the reception was under way. As I was putting some food on my plate, a family friend who was in line on the opposite side of the table glanced at me, then did a double take.

He stood there blinking, and I raised my eyebrows.

"I'm sorry," he said, shaking his head and blinking again. "But I thought you died."

CHAPTER SIXTY-ONE

THE PNEUMONIA CAME back with a vengeance during the three days I was out of the hospital. The day I got back to New Haven, I spiked a fever of 102, and my oncologist admitted me to the hospital again. The first night back in the hospital, I lay in bed and watched the clear drops of antibiotics drip through my IV, trying not to regret my choice to leave the hospital for a few days. What if I ended up dying not in spite of attending the wedding—but because of it? What if I'd foolishly gambled the last of my nine lives and lost?

I hadn't asked God for anything in a long time, except sometimes to take me home to be with Him when I was especially weary. But that night I remembered the man who had said, "I thought you died," and his words had a reverse psychological effect on me. Instead of resigning myself to what seemed like inevitable death, for the first time in months I became determined to live.

I remembered *The Message*'s translation of Romans 10:13: "Everyone who says, 'Help, God!' gets help."

I hadn't felt connected to God in forever, but that night I reached out to Him in the darkness and prayed with everything I had in me.

"Help, God." All night long, I prayed that prayer with every drop of antibiotics that trickled into my IV, like a medicinal rosary. One prayer for every drop. "Help, God."

As I watched the first streaks of morning light breaking through the dark wall of night sky, I pleaded with God for my life. "I don't want to die; I want to live. Please let me live."

When my pulmonologist came to see me later that morning, I gave him an ultimatum. "My twenty-ninth birthday is in two weeks, and I will not be celebrating it in the hospital. You have to get me better and discharge me, or I'm going to make a rope out of these bedsheets and climb out the window."

I felt relieved as my old determination emerged from months of despair. That afternoon, I sat on the edge of my bed and practiced the deep breathing exercises and gentle stretches the yoga instructor had tried to teach me the week before. Then, holding on to my IV pole for support, I walked to the nurses' station and back.

"Help, God," I whispered with every step. "Help, God. Help, God. Help."

CHAPTER SIXTY-TWO

I GOT OUT OF THE hospital the night before my birthday. I had made plans to sublet my apartment to a visiting Yale professor. He moved in the day before I was scheduled to fly to Portland, and Ian offered to let me stay in his guest room for my last night in New Haven.

We ate take-out chicken tikka masala from our favorite Indian restaurant, and then sipped cabernet while we sat side by side on the couch in his living room. It was the same couch where he'd lain next to me a year and a half earlier, when I'd cried at the thought of how a mastectomy would change our relationship. Never did I dream he would break up with me, or that now, on my last night in Connecticut, we'd end up discussing how we could repair our broken relationship while we lived on opposite coasts.

"What do you think?" he asked.

"I don't know. What do you want to do?" I asked, and I readjusted the felt cap covering my bald head. I still cared about him, and we shared a lot of beautiful memories, in spite of all the pain he'd put me through.

"I've missed you like crazy," he said. "I want to try again."

That night as I changed into pajamas in the guest bathroom, I smiled at the thought of Ian coming to visit me in Portland. Maybe we'd wake up tomorrow to find that cancer and chemo and radiation and the breakup were all a bad dream.

And then I looked down and saw a pregnancy test in the bottom of the bathroom trash can. It was negative. But still. It was a pregnancy test—and I'd never taken one in my life.

My heart started pounding, and my eyes filled with hot tears. *How could I have been so stupid? How had I come so close to giving him a second chance?*

I picked up the trash can and marched into his bedroom. He was lying on his stomach in the pitch-black room, nearly buried under a thick down comforter. I turned on the small lamp on his nightstand, and thrust the trash can near his head. "What's this?" I asked.

He turned onto his back, and rubbed his groggy eyes. "What's wrong, babe?" he asked.

"Don't call me babe," I hissed. And as I tried not to let the weight of his betrayal shatter me, I asked again, "What's this?"

He opened his eyes and stared at the used pregnancy test in the trash can, and a look of horror spread across his face.

"Oh, no. Oh *shit*," he said as he buried his face beneath his hands.

And then it all came out. While he'd been supposedly supporting me, his girlfriend, through cancer treatments, he'd been having sex with another woman. No wonder he'd seemed so distracted in the months after my mastectomy. No wonder he'd felt so far away. He hadn't just been working long hours; he'd been cheating on me with the barista who made his latte every morning at the local coffee shop. A girl who had real breasts—and a full head of hair.

"You weren't ever supposed to find out," he groaned. "You weren't ever supposed to know."

I sank to the edge of his bed and grabbed his shoulders with both hands. My angry tears spilled onto his bare chest as I shook him, and cried over and over again, "Wasn't I worth anything to you? You cheating bastard, wasn't I worth anything?"

CHAPTER SIXTY-THREE

IAN AND I DIDN'T say a word to each other as we drove to the airport the following morning. He pulled up to the curb in the Departures lane, and I yanked my suitcases from the backseat and slammed the door closed. *Don't cry, and don't look back,* I told myself as I hurried into the airport.

Once my plane was airborne, I tried to convince myself that it was actually a good thing I'd discovered Ian's secret. At least I could have a fresh start in a new city. At least I could have irrefutable closure that my life in New Haven—and any promise of a life with Ian in California—was over.

Once I let go of my failed past, I started planning future goals. I decided I was going to live in Portland for one year to give myself enough time and perspective for the emotional and physical scars to heal. Getting away from New Haven would give me the chance to hit the cosmic "reset" button before moving to Manhattan the following year to finish my degree at Columbia.

In the meantime, I was going to begin taking the five-year course of tamoxifen, a hormone-blocking medication that would significantly reduce my risk of a cancer recurrence.

I was going to start writing my story—because writing helped me process my experiences, and because crafting a narrative out of my losses was a way of redeeming the pain.

And I was going to try to find God again. Or maybe give Him the chance to find me? I still wasn't sure who had lost whom. When people from my church had prayed for me the night before my mastectomy, they had all told me to hold on to Jesus. And as hard as I'd clung to my faith in Him through the five surgeries and seven months of chemo and radiation, I still felt as if He or I—or maybe both of us—had let go.

CHAPTER SIXTY-FOUR

S HORTLY AFTER I arrived in Portland, I started working in an ER three days a week. I wore a wig to work every day, and didn't tell anyone where I'd been or what I'd just come through or even that I was still getting cancer treatments.

I rented a one-bedroom apartment and then bought a bed, a table and chairs, and a sofa. But I didn't hang anything on the walls because I told myself it was only temporary. I was just hiding out here for a year, and then everything was going to go back to normal. I was going to move back to the East Coast, finish my last few courses at Columbia, and start my career as a health reporter for a major news magazine. *It's not forever; it's just for now,* I said, studying my sparse apartment.

I started attending Imago Dei shortly after. For the first few months, I snuck into the back row after the service had started, wearing sunglasses to hide the tears I couldn't contain. And at the end of the service, while the worship band sang songs about God's unconditional love that prompts sinners' unconditional surrender, I knelt at the Communion table and wept some more. Every week as I knelt there, I unloaded my burdens and questions.

Why had God let this happen? Why would He do this to someone He loved when I wouldn't do it to someone I hated? Why had
He taken Libby instead of me? Why did He feel so far away?

As I returned to church week after week, without feeling any better and without uncovering any answers, I kept thinking about a
story from my childhood. When I was in elementary school, my parents took our family to the National Zoo in Washington, DC, and
somehow we managed to lose my younger brother Matthew, who
was in preschool.

When they realized he was gone, my parents began to panic. It
was a massive, crowded place and they couldn't remember where
they'd gotten separated from him. So we began to backtrack, visiting
the exhibits one by one, looking for Matthew.

We finally found him climbing a small tree outside of the monkey
cages. He was straddling a branch, singing to himself. When he saw
my parents, he dropped down out of the tree and smiled.

My parents hugged him in relief, but Matthew didn't seem panicked at all. My mom asked if he'd been scared, and Matthew
shook his head. "You always told me if I got lost to stay where I
was, and you would come find me," he said. "I *knew* you were going to find me."

As I fell into my new routine in Portland and prayed the same
prayer every week at the Communion table, I hoped God shared my
parents' views on what to do when you're lost. I hoped He was looking down from heaven saying, "I know you're lost. Just stay where
you are. I'll come find you." Church seemed as good a place as any to
encounter God—if He still existed, and if He still cared about finding me.

Living anonymously in a new city and wearing wigs and sunglasses most of the time, I felt as if I were in a witness protection

program, hiding out from the cancer that had tried to kill me. I thought I'd lost all there was to lose, and now I would live where cancer couldn't touch me, and God couldn't help but find me.

But instead, it was the other way around. For a long time, God felt absent, and it seemed as if cancer never left.

CHAPTER SIXTY-FIVE

DURING THE WEEK after the ER visit, Hadhi was still feeling under the weather. I tried to imagine how difficult it would be to feel sick, but still have to take care of five little ones. So that week I tried to go over frequently to help out with the girls so Hadhi could get some rest.

One morning I went over while the older three girls were at school. I told Hadhi I'd take Lelo and Chaki on an outing for a few hours so she could take a nap. I chased the girls around the house for twenty minutes before I finally got them to be still enough to put clothes on. Finally, I got them dressed and we were out the door.

The girls were still enamored of their pink and purple car seats. So when I told them they were going to go for a ride in my car, with their special seats, the girls were ecstatic.

They quickly climbed into their seats and let me buckle them in. We drove on back roads toward a neighborhood close to them that has a few shops and a park with a duck pond. Our drive took us past Reed College, a beautiful campus with expansive, manicured green lawns and stately red brick buildings.

Chaki was enthralled by the campus. As we drove by, she pressed her nose to the window and said, "Is that your house!?"

"No, baby," I said. "That's a school for really big kids. It's called a college."

"I want to go to your house!" Chaki yelled.

"But that's not my house," I said. "That's a college. When you're big enough to go to school, you can study hard and do your homework, and someday you and Lelo can go to college. How about that?"

As we kept driving toward the coffee shop, I heard the two of them chattering in the backseat. Chaki leaned over and whispered to Lelo, "We go to college."

Lelo whispered back, "But first we need backpacks."

We parked in front of Starbucks, and went inside to get treats. At first I made the mistake of asking them which pastry they wanted from the case. "I want that one. And that one. And that one. And that one," Lelo said. "I want *all* the yum-yums."

I realized it was too much to ask them to choose one, so I made the choice for them. I bought one chocolate chip cookie for them to eat, and a cup of water for them to drink. I got myself a coffee, and then we sat down at a table by the window to enjoy our treats.

It was fascinating to watch them take in their surroundings. I realized that just getting them out of the house and letting them see everyday life in America would go a long way toward helping them acclimate to the new culture.

They got to see other little kids coming in with their parents, behaving well in the coffee shop, talking quietly to their parents and siblings, and sharing drinks and cookies. I was glad for the Somali girls to be able to see in person the values I'd been trying to describe to them when I said things like, "Share. Be nice. Don't hit."

After we finished our snacks, I took them to the bathroom. Lelo was fine—she used the toilet, flushed, and washed her hands without needing any prompting. But Chaki was a different story. The bathroom was so much bigger, brighter, and cleaner than the one at home, at first she didn't realize it was even the same thing.

When Lelo flushed and the sound reverberated loudly against the tiles, Chaki freaked out. She started crying and trying to climb up my leg. I picked her up, and she buried her head against my neck. "I have scared! I have scared!" she screamed. I tried not to laugh as I assured her that the toilet was not going to devour her.

After they used the bathroom, I bundled them up in their jackets, and we drove to the park to see the ducks. They ran around for a while, trying unsuccessfully to capture one of the birds with their bare hands, telling me that they wanted to take a duck home as a pet.

Lelo was disappointed when I told her that, first of all, people weren't allowed to take ducks from the park, and second, the apartment complex manager probably wouldn't appreciate them having a quacking duck in their small apartment.

A little while later, I put the girls back in their car seats and we started driving to their house.

"We go to your house?" they kept saying.

"Not today," I said. "We're going back to *your* house."

"No, not my house. *Your* house," Lelo said as if I hadn't understood what she was saying. "I want to go to *your* house."

When we pulled into the parking lot of their apartment, Lelo recognized where we were. "What the *hell*?" she yelled. "This is my house!"

"I told you we were going back to your house," I said, trying not to laugh at the indignant look on her face. "Your mommy would miss you if we didn't come home."

"I hate my house. I go to your house," she insisted.

Chaki chimed in. "Hate my house," she said. "I go in my chair to your house."

"Sorry, guys, not today."

I unbuckled them, but they refused to get out of their seats. When I tried to pick them up, they held on to the armrests and were immovable. It was a very successful sit-in, which ended when I had to go get Hadhi to help me. She came out and yelled something in Somali, and then the girls quickly got out of my car and, ignoring my attempts to hug them good-bye, ran inside their apartment and shut the door.

CHAPTER SIXTY-SIX

HADHI WAS STILL sick the following Saturday. I wanted to take the girls for a few hours so she could get some sleep, but I knew I couldn't handle all five of them by myself—and they wouldn't all fit in my little car.

So I enlisted the help of my friend Stephanie to take the girls to Chuck E. Cheese. I had never been, but there was one close to their house. Eating pizza and playing video games seemed like good indoor activities for a cold, rainy night.

I arrived at the apartment before Stephanie and helped the girls put on their clothes, coats, and shoes. Hadhi had resisted my efforts to use hangers and closet organizers. So while their clothes were (mostly) clean, they were stored in garbage bags in the closet. Whenever the girls wanted to get dressed, they would blindly reach into a bag and put on whatever they happened to find, even if it didn't match, or didn't fit.

So, dressed in mismatched shirts, stained pants, and untied shoes without any socks, the five girls stood with me in the hall and declared they were ready to go.

When Stephanie showed up, we loaded the three older girls into her car, and the two littlest girls into their car seats in the back of my car. We drove less than five minutes down the road to Chuck E. Cheese, parked our cars, and walked inside.

It hadn't occurred to me that because it was a rainy Saturday evening, every parent in Portland would bring their stir-crazy kids there. It was a madhouse.

We checked in with the hostess and asked for a table for seven. She told me it would be about fifteen minutes, and disappeared into the restaurant to make room. While we stood in the lobby, I pointed to a large picture of a smiling mouse above the entrance.

"Do you know who that is?" I asked Chaki.

"It's Mitty Mouse!" she cried.

"Well, it is *a* mouse," I said, "but not Mickey."

"How about you, Lelo? Do you want to guess?"

"It's Justeen Beaver!" she exclaimed. "I really like Justeen."

I laughed, and then explained that we were not at Mickey Mouse's or Justin Bieber's; we were at Chuck E. Cheese's. Which was how, for the rest of the night, they ended up calling him Chuck E. Jesus.

When we were seated at our table a few minutes later, we decided that Stephanie would take the three older girls to buy tickets so they could play some games, and I'd take the two younger girls to order the food. We got two cheese pizzas, a vegetable tray, and cups of water.

I divvied up the food, and the girls dug in, exclaiming how much they loved pizza. "I like your *fooood*," Chaki kept saying as she licked cheese and sauce from her fingertips. "I really like your *fooood*."

They had each polished off two pieces and were about to get thirds when I pointed out that none of them had touched the vegetables on their plate. I made them eat one bite of each vegetable before they could have any more pizza, which they protested but in the end tried to obey.

After the pizza was gone, they each ate a small cup of chocolate ice cream. And then we cleared the table and got ready to play some of the arcade games. Sadaka pulled on my hand. I leaned down and she whispered, "I have to pee."

"And me, too," Chaki said.

I took them both by the hand and we walked to the bathroom. Lelo came running in behind us. "Me, too!" she said.

When we got into the bathroom, I told them that all the stalls were full, and we'd have to wait our turn to go potty. Lelo started squirming. A minute later, she was running through the bathroom, hitting the closed stall doors with her fist, yelling, "My poop is coming out! My poop is coming out!"

The doors opened quickly and several mothers, who were holding the hands of neatly dressed little girls whose outfits were not stained or mismatched or smelly, emerged from the stalls. They glared at me, and then at my little ragtag army of girls. The Somali girls were unaware of the atmosphere in the bathroom, but the mothers' silent stares made me intensely uncomfortable, and made me want to defend the girls' curry-stained clothes, broken English, and lack of social skills. But instead, I silently waited for the girls to finish using the bathroom, and then I helped them wash and dry their hands.

At the end of the night, we were attempting to get everyone's jackets on and get them to the cars when Chaki escaped and ran out of the front door that a woman in a beautiful long wool coat was holding open. Instead of reaching for Chaki, she simply stood there and watched as I frantically dashed out the door to grab her.

As I was running past the woman, she looked me up and down and sniffed, "Is that *your* little boy?"

CHAPTER SIXTY-SEVEN

I HAD LIVED IN Portland for only a few weeks when I got the call from my OB/GYN that my ovaries had shut down, and as he put it, *I might as well have a hysterectomy.* I went to Karina's house so I wouldn't have to process the news alone. After she'd put the boys to bed that evening, we sat on the couch talking. "Sarah, my heart is just breaking for you," she said as she hugged me.

That night as I lay in my bed alone, staring at the ceiling, I asked God, "Is Your heart breaking, too?"

Since my initial diagnosis, I'd had dueling images of God in my head, and I couldn't reconcile the two. There was the God that Paul wrote about as a commanding officer, when he said, "Endure suffering along with me, as a good soldier of Christ Jesus" (2 Timothy 2:3 NLT).

And then there was the God that Matthew described as a Father who wanted to give good gifts to His children.

When God seemed to be silent, I couldn't tell if He was a military officer who was pushing me until I either broke or became stronger, or if He was the loving Father who was aware of every tear I cried, whose heart was breaking for me. But if He *was* that loving

Father, and if He *did* know the pain I was in, why wouldn't He do something? I'd posed that question to the hospital chaplain when I was in sepsis, and she left the room and never came back.

A few days after the chaplain left, an oncology social worker from the hospital came to my room to see how I was doing. I was choking on tears before I could finish asking the question, "If God loves me, how can He let me hurt this much?"

"What do you think?" she asked.

"I have no idea," I said. "I've decided that either God doesn't exist, or He's terribly angry with me, or there's something I'm missing about His character that lets Him love His children but allows them to suffer at the same time."

I asked her what she thought, and she launched into her own theory. "I think God is like a giant and we're like ants," she said. "I think He tramples some of us, but not because He's mean, it's just because we are unfortunate enough to be in His way. I think suffering is a random accident," she said. Then she patted my hand and walked away, leaving me to wonder what comfort I was supposed to find in randomness.

CHAPTER SIXTY-EIGHT

AFTER TAKING CHAKI and Lelo to the park, and then taking all of the girls to Chuck E. Cheese, I'd brought them back to the apartment to find Hadhi relaxed and well rested. Having a few hours to herself when she could clean the apartment, shower, and take a nap had done wonders for her countenance.

So I kept going back once or twice a week while the older girls were in school to pick up Chaki and Lelo for a few hours so Hadhi could have a break. A few days after Chuck E. Cheese, I went over to the apartment and got Lelo and Chaki dressed. They were especially wound up that day—I had to chase them around the apartment for twenty minutes before I got them to sit still enough to put their shoes on.

Once I got them in the car, they had a hard time sitting still in their car seats. They kept wiggling out of the restraints, until I finally had to pull into a gas station and tell them that if they didn't keep their seat belts on and sit still in their car seats, we'd have to turn around and go home.

They finally cooperated, and we drove to Starbucks to get hot chocolate on the way to the park. As we walked into the coffee shop,

I was carrying Chaki, and Lelo was walking next to me, holding my hand.

I sat Chaki down on the counter while we ordered two small kids' hot chocolates and one coffee. As I was reaching into my purse for my wallet, I saw out of the corner of my eye that Chaki had her hand in the tip jar. She was taking the change and putting it into her coat pocket. When I looked up at her and called her name, she didn't look startled or guilty; she just smiled at me and kept putting fistfuls of change into her pockets.

"Money!" she said. "Do you want some money?"

I realized that she had no concept of a tip jar—she thought the tip money was there for the taking.

"That money's not for us," I said as I helped her unload her pockets. "That's money we give to the people who work here to say thank you."

She flashed a grin at the barista behind the counter. "Thank you!" she said.

"Awwww, she's so cute," the barista said, and the other two baristas came over to say hi to the girls, too.

And then Lelo melted down. For no apparent reason, she threw herself on the floor in front of the counter and started yelling. "You broke my leg, Sahara! You broke my leg!"

"Lelo, get up," I said quietly but sternly.

"I can't walk!" she yelled. "My leg is broken! My leg is broken!"

I crouched down next to her. "Lelo, I did not break your leg. I didn't even touch you. Now stop yelling, act like a big girl, and come drink your hot chocolate."

I was suddenly aware that all the people in the coffee shop were looking at us. I thought of how the situation must look to an outsider. The girls were a different ethnicity, wearing skirts and Muslim headdresses. What if someone thought I was a kidnapper? Or that I really was hurting them and trying to break their legs?

I wanted to turn around and defend myself against these imaginary accusations.

It's okay.

They belong with me.

I love these girls and I take really good care of them.

They're from Somalia and they don't get out much.

But instead, I absorbed the stares and kept trying to get Lelo up off the floor. And just then, she changed tactics. Instead of screaming about her broken leg, she yelled, "Hey! Hey! That's nasty! Somebody peed and pooped and farted!"

The coffee shop didn't smell any different from any other Starbucks; she was just yelling whatever shocking things popped into her head. I knew I had to get her to the car *now*, before she started yelling the expansive vocabulary of obscenities she had picked up from her older sisters, who had learned the words on the playground at school.

In the meantime, three-year-old Chaki was doing great. She was standing at the counter, winking at the baristas and conversing with them. I put the hot chocolates in a carrier and gave them to Chaki. Then I swooped Lelo up in my arms, and we made our exit.

Once we got to the car, it took me ten minutes—including one mad dash to try to keep her from running into traffic—before I had Lelo calm enough to put her into her car seat and fasten the seat belt.

After I dropped them off at the apartment, I started thinking about how to help them acclimate better to American social skills. It was too daunting for me to accomplish by myself. There was no way I could fit all five girls in my little car, let alone give them one-on-one attention and explanations of their new culture.

And that was when I decided that the girls needed Big Sisters. Like the Big Brothers Big Sisters program, we could pair each of the girls with a woman as a mentor and friend. Public meltdowns might still happen, but they'd be easier with a one-to-one ratio.

CHAPTER SIXTY-NINE

KARINA, BETSY, KARRIE, and our friend Kristin agreed to be Big Sisters to the Invisible Girls. We decided that once a month we'd each take our little Somali sister on a one-on-one outing to do anything from going to the library to running errands to playing in the park.

I signed up for Lelo, since she had the most behavioral issues. I picked her up one February afternoon, and we drove to the park. I thought it might be easier to get her to cooperate indoors if she had the chance to run out her energy out-of-doors first.

We parked across the street from the park, I buttoned up her coat and gave her my mittens, and then we ran wherever her little legs would take her. Around the baseball diamond, up over the small wooden bridge that spanned the creek, past the ducks and geese, then back through a group of sleeping ducks that were trying to mind their own business, then down the hill to the slide and the swings.

And then Lelo spotted the seesaw. She ran up to it. "What's this!?" she asked.

"It's a seesaw," I said.

"A see-it-tall?" she asked.

"Close." I laughed.

"How do you do it?" she asked.

I set her down on one side of the seesaw, then made a big show of running around to the other end, sitting down, and bringing my side down until she was sitting high in the air.

"Lelo, I'm going to send you to the moon!" I teased her.

"To the moon!" she yelled, giggling.

We seesawed for a while, and then she decided she'd rather go terrorize the ducks. After we ran through the ducks one more time, I put her back in her car seat, and we drove to my favorite used book shop in Portland—a quaint old house piled from floor to ceiling with books, filled with the pleasant smell of burning wood from the fireplace in the main room.

We sat in the kids' room for a while, and I let her rummage through the books. I told her she could pick out three books (I let her talk me into five), and then we went to the front to pay. When we were halfway to the register, I realized that she'd left her jacket on the floor, so I went back to get it while she kept walking toward the front of the shop. I was in the other room when I heard her drop the stack of books and yell, "Hey, that's nasty! Sahara, it's *nasty*!"

I groaned. Not another meltdown.

I found her in front of the register, staring at a display of black-and-white greeting cards. One of the cards had a picture of a naked male Rodin sculpture.

"Nasty!" she yelled again, pointing to the picture.

I quickly turned it backward and said, "Is that better?"

She nodded and, to my relief, quickly recovered. She handed a few dollars to the woman behind the counter, and we got her bundled up to walk back to the car. As we were leaving, I leaned down and said, "What do you say to that nice lady?"

"Thank you for giving to me these books!" Lelo called over her shoulder.

As she held a stack of Beatrix Potter books in one arm, she held my hand with the other. While we were walking the three blocks to my car, she chattered, "Sahara, are you my Big Sister?"

"Yes, baby," I said. "I'm your Big Sister."

"Do you love me?" she asked.

"Yes, baby, I love you *so* much."

She looked content with my answer. As I buckled her into her seat for the drive home, she said, "Sahara, do you know what? I love you, too."

CHAPTER SEVENTY

A FEW DAYS AFTER my outing with Lelo, three of the other Big Sisters went over to the apartment to take their Little Sisters out for their monthly outing. But when they got to the apartment, something wasn't right. There was a man at the apartment that Hadhi kept referring to as "my husband." When my friends asked if they could take their little siblings out for a few hours, the man said no. Hadhi explained that they had decided to move their family to Seattle, where she had a female relative that she referred to as "my sister."

The Big Sisters stayed for an hour or so and played with the girls at the apartment, and then Hadhi asked them to leave.

I heard about the strange event later that night. My mind was spinning with questions. Was Hadhi's estranged, abusive husband back with the family? Were the girls okay? I thought Hadhi had told me she had no sisters in America, so who was this woman in Seattle? Why were they moving? What would I do without them?

I tried to call Hadhi the next morning, but her phone was off. After I finished my shift at the clinic the next evening, I drove over to the apartment. The lights were off, the door was locked, and it was completely silent.

I went back to my car, climbed inside, locked the doors, and tried to think.

They had never not been home in the evening. If they weren't in the apartment, where else could they be? What if they'd moved away already? How would I find them? As I turned out of the parking lot and started driving home, I decided I was jumping too far ahead. I'd try to get in touch with Hadhi the next morning. They had to be somewhere.

I called Hadhi's cell phone every day for a week, but every time I called, it was off and I couldn't leave a voice mail. I drove over to the apartment at different times on three different days, and each time the door was locked and no one was home.

And so, for about a week, I was convinced that the Invisible Girls had disappeared. In that empty space, a lot of thoughts ran through my head. I wondered what had happened to make them bolt like that. I wondered if that man really was her husband, and if so, how he had found them. I wondered if Hadhi and the girls were safe. And I wondered how in the world I could find them if they'd moved already.

I knew their lease wasn't up for another six months and they probably didn't have enough know-how, let alone financial resources, to make arrangements to break the lease. So it was doubtful that the apartment manager would have a forwarding address for them. The only other bill they had was through the electric company, but did Hadhi know enough English to have a phone conversation about turning off the power and giving them a forwarding address? Could I track them through DHS? Would they give me the family's information if I couldn't prove my relationship to them?

I thought about the girls trying to find me, but quickly concluded that this would be impossible. They didn't have my cell phone number written down—and I was worried Hadhi had tossed her prepaid cell phone where my number was saved. They didn't know my address. They didn't even know my last name.

They only knew me as Sahara—their American sister who brought them pizza and helped them with their homework and danced like a crazy person around the living room, just to make them smile.

CHAPTER SEVENTY-ONE

A WEEK LATER, I hadn't been able to contact the family or find out where they'd gone. I decided I'd go by the apartment one more time before concluding that they'd moved away. I drove to the apartment, parked, and walked up to the front door. My heart skipped a beat when I heard little girls clamoring and singing inside. Hallelujah, they were home!

I knocked on the door, and Fahari answered. The other girls squealed and came running to me. The weight of their collective hugs pulled me down to the floor, and we fell into a giggling heap.

"Where have you been?" Fahari demanded.

"I've been coming every day to find you," I said. "Where have *you* been?"

"At school," she said.

"Where has your mom been?" I asked her.

She shrugged, and I let the question drop for the moment. She explained that Hadhi had gone to the store and left them home by themselves. "Will you stay with us?" she asked.

"Of course," I said. "I'll stay until your mom gets back."

The six of us made our way to the stack of mattresses in the bedroom. Abdallah picked the animated version of *Alice in Wonderland* from a pile of movies on the floor, and we sat together watching the movie.

And then the front door opened—and I realized in our excitement to hug and watch a movie, we'd neglected to lock it. The girls went running into the hall to greet the person I thought was Hadhi. But instead of hearing her familiar voice, I heard a man's voice barking commands in Somali.

Abdallah and Fahari started talking back to him, and I heard them say my name a few times. Sadaka came running into the bedroom, grabbed my hand, and led me to the closet. She leaned down and whispered, "It's our dad. He doesn't want to see you." And then she closed the closet door and left the room.

I sat in the dark, on a pile of dank clothes, my heart pounding. The Monster was back. The man who had abused Hadhi and locked her and the girls in the house without food or clothes. The man the Department of Justice had said was a threat to the family. That man was in the hall now, with these precious little girls.

I wondered if he'd changed since he'd left. Maybe he was more peaceful, kinder. Then again, maybe he was angrier and more violent than before. Who could tell? I had pepper spray in the glove box of my car, but it was across the parking lot and would do me no good now.

I thought about the exits from the room. The only option besides going through the hall and out the front door was a small window on the far side of the bedroom. I could make a run for it and crawl out the window, and get to my car that way. But what about the girls? I decided I couldn't leave them alone with a man whose character was so uncertain. And so I stayed. I sat in the closet and prayed for him and for the girls and for me.

It felt like I was hiding in there for an eternity, though it was probably less than fifteen minutes. I heard footsteps coming down the hall, then the bedroom door opening. And then the closet door opened, and a short African man wearing a suit that was several sizes too big for him stood there, staring down at me. I looked up at him without saying anything, and flashed a weak smile, willing myself to be small and calm and nonthreatening.

"You are Sarah?" he asked in a thick accent.

I nodded.

"I heard about you," he said.

I nodded again. "You have a beautiful family," I said. "I love your girls."

The front door opened, and I heard Hadhi's voice. Her estranged husband muttered something to me, then walked out of the room. I heard him arguing with Hadhi in the hall, and again I heard my name inserted into the conversation. Hadhi came into the room, took my hand, and pulled me to my feet.

CHAPTER SEVENTY-TWO

H I, HADHI," I said as she took my hand and pulled me up. I shook my legs to get rid of the pins-and-needles sensation in my feet. How long had I been squatting in the back of that closet?

She hugged me and said, "Sorry, sorry, sorry, Sarah." We walked to the living room, and I sat there on the floor with the girls while Hadhi and her husband sat on the couch.

With Fahari translating, Hadhi explained that after she got sick during the winter, she'd been so run down and desperate for help with the children, she'd called her husband and asked him to come help her.

He had been living and working in a town about forty-five minutes away. He'd ridden the bus over to the apartment several times in the past few weeks. When Hadhi told him about the family's financial situation, he had decided that she and the girls needed to move in with her relatives, who had recently arrived in Seattle. Like Hadhi, they didn't have much money to spare, but if the two families shared one apartment, they would at least have enough money for clothes and utilities and other expenses that Hadhi struggled to afford.

"You're moving to Seattle?" I asked.

Hadhi nodded.

"When?" I asked.

"Monday," she said.

I looked at her husband. "Are you going to Seattle, too?" I asked.

He shook his head and explained he was going to stay where he was and keep working. At least that was something, I decided. But still—today was Thursday. I had plans to go camping with friends for the weekend. I was coming back on Sunday afternoon, and the Invisible Girls were moving on Monday.

"Where are you going to stay?" I asked Hadhi. "Do you know your address?"

She shook her head, but took her cell phone from her waistband and dialed the number. She handed the phone to me, and an African woman named Amine whose English was much better than Hadhi's answered the phone.

I explained who I was, and asked if I could have her address so I could come visit the family in Seattle. Amine gave me her address and cell phone number, and then hung up. I wrote the information in a small notebook, and then put it back in my purse. I didn't know what else to do, except make plans to say good-bye.

"I'll come see you and say good-bye on Sunday night. We'll have a pizza party and give each other lots and lots of hugs, okay?"

The girls nodded eagerly.

As I pulled out of the parking lot, I looked in the rearview mirror and saw the girls standing at the door, waving to me. I thought about all the memories and adventures and sorrows and stories we'd shared together.

A song called "Just a Dream" came on the radio as I was driving home, and I remembered the surreal-but-beautiful six months I'd spent with the Invisible Girls. This dream of unexpected love and healing had saved my life. And I dreaded the thought of waking up.

CHAPTER SEVENTY-THREE

I GOT BACK FROM my trip late Sunday afternoon, and without going home to change or unpack, I went to the store to get supplies for the last meal I'd have with the Invisible Girls before they left town the next day.

I bought two cheese take-and-bake pizzas and some bright floral paper plates, napkins, and cups. The other Big Sisters were coming to the party, too, but I went over to the apartment first because I wanted the chance to get the food ready. And I wanted some time alone with them to say good-bye.

My eyes welled with tears as I pulled up in front of the apartment complex. As glad as I was that they hadn't suddenly vanished and that I'd had the opportunity to get their new address and say good-bye, it was difficult to have to walk through the process of seeing them go.

I turned off my car and sat there for a few minutes, giving myself a pep talk. *You can't let them see you cry,* I told myself. *Make this about a new opportunity and an exciting adventure for them—it's not about you.*

As I got out of my car, I decided to make the night a celebration of the memories we had together, rather than about what we were all losing. *You can cry later,* I promised myself as I stood on their doorstep and took a deep breath.

I reveled in the chance to repeat our old routine one last time. I rapped my signature knock on the front door. While I waited, I heard the neighbor's dogs barking next door. Then I heard shouts of delight from the girls inside their apartment, and the patter of bare feet against the hardwood floors as they ran toward the door.

I heard Hadhi tell them all to stand back as she fiddled with the stubborn locks. And before she could get the door open, I saw two sets of chocolate brown eyes peering through the mail slot at me, and then two small hands reaching through it—Lelo and Chaki trying to be the first ones to touch me.

Hadhi opened the door and I hugged her—and saw behind her the sparse living room that was empty except for a pile of black garbage bags. All of their belongings fit into one little corner of one little room.

The girls clamored to hug me, and I laughed and told them I needed to set the pizzas down first. I went into the kitchen, turned on the oven, and put the pizzas inside. Then I sat on the floor in the living room with Chaki and Lelo in my lap, and Fahari and Sadaka sitting next to me.

They told me about their family in Seattle, about how sad they were to say good-bye to their friends here, about how much they would miss me.

And then I realized that Abdallah was missing. I asked the girls where she was, and they told me she was in the bedroom. I found her sitting in the dark hallway just outside the bedroom door, her back propped against the wall and her knobby knees pulled up to her chest. Her arms were resting on the tops of her knees, and she was sobbing into them.

I sat down on the floor next to her and put my arm around her shoulders. She climbed into my lap, and then she wrapped her arms tightly around my neck, buried her face against my shoulder, and wept.

"Shhh," I said, stroking her hair. "Shhh."

When the tears relented, I pulled her away from me so I could look her in the eye. "I have your address, so I'm going to visit you all in Seattle, okay?"

She nodded.

"No matter where you go, I promise I will always love you, and I will always find you." She took my palm and pressed it against her scarred cheek, and her tears began again.

CHAPTER SEVENTY-FOUR

M Y TIME WITH ABDALLAH was cut short by the deafening sound of smoke alarms. As usual, whenever the oven was on for more than a few minutes, it got smoky and set off all the smoke detectors in the apartment.

The girls took off their headscarves and ran to the detectors in the hall and the bedroom and fanned them while I went to check on the pizza. Chaki followed me into the kitchen and pulled at my leg. "Up," she pleaded. "Pick me up."

I put her on my hip while I set out the napkins and cups and plates. Lelo asked for juice. Sadaka ran into the kitchen and told me she was *starving* and asked when the pizza was going to be ready. It was just the same as ever. The same interactions and grins and teasing as always. Only this time, it was like everything was going in slow motion, and I was savoring every second, knowing it was going to be the last time I'd see them for a long while.

I took the pizza from the oven and poured juice for all the girls. And then, while we were waiting for the pizza to cool, I took Fahari into the bedroom where Hadhi was packing. Since Fahari spoke the best English of all of them, I wanted to make sure she was there to translate what I was saying, and to remember—even if everyone else forgot.

I took an index card out of my pocket and showed it to Hadhi. The week before, when I thought they'd moved away already, I realized they didn't have my name or contact information written down. So before I came over that evening, I'd spelled it all out on an index card. I gave it to Hadhi to put in her purse, which served as the filing cabinet for all of their important papers and documents.

I showed it to Fahari, too. "This is my name," I said. "Here's my address, my phone number, and my e-mail. If you need anything, *anything*, you call me anytime, okay?"

Fahari and Hadhi nodded. I gave Hadhi the card, and she tucked it away in her purse.

As I was going over my contact information with Hadhi, her husband showed up. He had ridden the bus for an hour so he could come and say good-bye to his family. He wore an oversized winter coat, stained khakis, and a baseball cap that was a few sizes too big for his head. As he sat in the corner of the living room silently munching on a slice of pizza, he seemed more defeated than domineering. When he'd finished eating, he waved to the girls and left without saying a word.

The other Big Sisters showed up a few minutes later. We sat in a circle on the floor and I prayed out loud for each of the girls by name, that God would continue to love and protect them. We ate pizza and vegetables and fruit, and drank cups of SunnyD.

Lelo sat in my lap and played with my hair, which, two years after chemo, was now down to my shoulders. I remembered her voice months ago, when I'd just started coming over to the apartment. *Seeet down. Seeet down. I want to seet in your yap.*

Before dinner was over, Hadhi's cell phone rang. She answered it, and talked for a few minutes in Somali. And then she told me, "My sister's coming now."

"Now?" I asked. "Tonight?"

Hadhi nodded. They were moving tonight. In a few minutes, they'd all be gone.

Karina had gotten each of the girls a matching ring and necklace to remind them that we were going to love and pray for them from a distance. Each of us Big Sisters got to put the jewelry on our little sister and hug her and tell her she was *so* special. I quickly packed up the leftover food and put it in a bag for them to eat in the car. And then we waited.

A few days before, my friend and I had discussed the movie *Life Is Beautiful*, a story about a Jewish couple and their young son who are sent to a Nazi concentration camp during World War II.

The second half of the movie chronicles the story of the father and his young son living in the camp together. In the end, the father tries to escape with his son and they are caught. He is able to stash his son in a corner, out of sight from the guards, but he is not so lucky. The guards grab him and take him away to execute him.

When the father realizes his son can see him from his hiding place, the father decides to put on a show for him. Even though he knows he is being led to his death, he flashes his son an absurd grin, and then does an exaggerated goose step until he's out of sight. And then, off camera, there's a gunshot followed by silence.

My friend said that some reviewers thought the scene was ridiculous, that it was unrealistic for a man who should have been experiencing fear and dread at that moment to act so silly.

I told him I thought that was one of the most beautiful parts of the movie. Because, really, what wouldn't a father do to try to secure the future happiness and sanity of his son?

I thought of that conversation when Sadaka came up to me and began singing her favorite Justin Bieber song. While we were waiting for her relatives to come pick them up, she grabbed my hands and I danced with her, exaggerating my movements and expressions to make her giggle. The silliness belied my sadness, but it was worth it to see her smile. A few minutes later, two Somali women arrived and began to carry the black garbage bags out to their vans.

Suddenly, it was time to say good-bye. I hugged Sadaka, Chaki, and Fahari without crying. And then Abdallah came to me with tears in her eyes and held her arms out to me. When I hugged her, I started to cry. I wiped the tears away quickly, and tried to force a smile. I didn't want her to know how sad their departure made me.

"You know I love you, baby," I said.

She flashed a timid smile. "I love you, too, Sahara."

And then it was time to say good-bye to Lelo, my little shadow. I knelt down and reached out to her. She giggled and ran to me and gave me a hug. "I love you *so* much," I told her through my tears. Finally, I hugged Hadhi. And then I left.

I got in my car and started driving, tears freely flowing now that I was alone. I tried to reassure myself that Seattle wasn't the end of the world; I could see them again. I tried to remember that God had brought them to Portland and into my life, and surely He would continue to take care of them even if they moved away. But still.

Somehow while I was aimlessly driving on the rainy Portland streets, these words comforted me:

It's the same old love song; only now it will be played to a different tune.

It's not the end of the Invisible Girls' story—it's just the start of Chapter Two.

And with that thought in mind, I pointed my car east, and headed home.

CHAPTER SEVENTY-FIVE

I T WASN'T UNTIL HADHI and the girls moved away that I fully realized what they had become to me. In the six months I knew them in Portland, they had become my dear friends, my adopted family, and my writing muse. And then, in the middle of the night, they packed up everything they owned into a pile of garbage bags, loaded up into two vans driven by their female relatives, and vanished.

I fell into a deep sadness after they left, feeling an aching void. My arms, which had been unexpectedly filled with precious little girls, were suddenly empty. I kept reminding myself, "It's not the end of the story; it's just the start of Chapter Two."

I talked to Hadhi and the girls on the phone a few times a week. As usual, when they called me, they didn't know how to leave a voice mail; I would just look at my phone and see that I'd missed fifteen calls from them over a ten-minute period.

When I called them, they passed the phone around until I'd gotten to talk to all of them. Their English was still limited, and talking over the phone was even more difficult than talking in person because I couldn't point to objects or act out words when their vocabulary failed. But they were able to tell me that they were having fun playing with their cousins, that they'd started school, and best of all—they got to ride on a school bus. In Portland they'd lived less than a mile from school, so they'd had to walk back and forth.

One evening my phone rang, and I picked it up. Fahari was on the other end. In adolescent concern that expressed itself as anger, she demanded, "Where have you been? I *miss* you." She started to cry.

"Sweetheart, I miss you, too," I said. "And I pray for you and your mom and your sisters every night before I go to sleep."

"We tried to get you to come," Fahari continued. "We called nine-one-one for help."

"What!?"

"We call nine-one-one and tell them to bring Sahara to Seattle. And I also say, tell her to come with ten pizzas."

"What did they say?" I asked.

"They very angry," she said. "They say, don't call us for that."

"You shouldn't call nine-one-one unless it's an emergency," I reminded Fahari.

At the end of the conversation, I promised to come visit them in Seattle soon. As I hung up the phone, I laughed at the thought of the dispatcher taking an emergency plea to send me to Seattle. With ten pizzas.

CHAPTER SEVENTY-SIX

Six months after I arrived in Portland, I was kneeling at the Communion table at the front of the church asking God the same questions I'd been asking for months. "Who are You? Where are You? And how could You do this to someone You love?" As I was kneeling there in silence, I remembered a night years before, when I was working as a phlebotomist to earn money for grad school.

One night I got called to Pediatrics to draw blood from a five-year-old girl who was being admitted with newly diagnosed diabetes. The nurses called me so I could draw blood off her IV instead of having to stick her with a needle a second time.

I walked into the room to introduce myself to the patient and her parents, and I immediately recognized the patient's mom, who was sitting in bed with her little girl. She was a physician on the hospital staff that I had often seen rounding on her patients while I was doing blood draws on the floors.

As the doctor stood against the wall watching, we strapped her daughter onto a papoose board, and started her IV. When the needle went into her arm, the little girl shrieked. As I collected her blood into vials to take to the lab, she kept screaming. After a few minutes of crying without seeing any results, she lifted her head off the table and screamed, "MOMMY! I'M IN PAIN!"

I watched the doctor's face, and noted the tears that welled up in her eyes as she watched her daughter continue to struggle against the restraints. But to her credit, she kept her distance and let us finish the procedure. The moment we were done, the doctor undid the restraints, scooped her daughter up in her arms, and rocked her until she fell asleep.

I thought about the paradox of that doctor. The mother in her loved her daughter, and wanted her to be as healthy and pain-free as possible. But the doctor in her knew that the very best thing for the little girl was an IV that could provide life-saving insulin and fluids.

And so, even though it caused her child pain, because the doctor knew it was ultimately in her child's best interest, she allowed us to inflict pain that the little girl could not understand. But at the soonest possible moment, she was there to pick her daughter up and carry her away from the pain.

And then I thought about the paradox of God. How was it possible that He could seem so far away and yet promise, "I will never leave you nor forsake you"? How could life hurt so much when He promised to give me "a future and a hope"?

In light of the woman who was simultaneously a mother and a physician, I began to see God as both my Father and the Great Physician. He was the infinitely loving, infinitely wise parent standing against the Procedure Room wall of life, watching me suffer as tears welled up in His eyes. He was waiting for the moment when the trial had finished its work in my life, ready to pick me up the second it was done and carry me home.

That was the last time I asked, *Where is God when I'm hurting?*

Because that day I heard the answer. *He's right here. And He's been here all along.*

I took Communion and then walked back to my seat. With hope and relief rising in my chest, I lifted my hands to heaven as the worship band sang,

> *The love of God is greater far*
> *Than tongue or pen can ever tell.*
> *It goes beyond the highest star*
> *And reaches to the lowest hell.*

For months I had been waiting to be found. And now I realized that all this time, in this lowest hell, through every heartbreak, and in each cry of pain, I had never been lost.

CHAPTER SEVENTY-SEVEN

AFTER A YEAR OF low-key existence in Portland, I was determined to reenter my East Coast life. I e-mailed the dean at Columbia and picked courses for the next semester. I applied for a job at a breast cancer center just outside Manhattan and was invited for an interview.

Perfect, I thought as I packed my suitcase to go back to New York for a long weekend. I was going to figure out a job and a place to live, finish the remaining coursework at Columbia, and get back on track to be a health reporter for a major news magazine.

I flew into JFK, and took a cab to a hotel near Grand Central Station. I had plans to experience quintessential New York for the weekend—a visit to Times Square, a Broadway show, lunch at Tavern on the Green, dinner at 21 Club.

But it was not as fun as I'd anticipated. As soon as I glimpsed Manhattan from the plane, I began to feel anxious. I spent the weekend taking deep breaths, repeating soothing mantras, and whispering short prayers, trying to fend off a major panic attack. I hardly slept for the three nights I was there. On Monday morning, I took the train to Connecticut and interviewed to be the clinical director of a breast cancer center.

The breast surgeon explained that my job would be to coordinate patients' care and organize multimillion-dollar fund-raising events attended by socialites in Manhattan and Greenwich. It was an incredible opportunity. But on the train ride back from Connecticut to my hotel, I leaned my head against the window and sighed. If this job was so perfect, if it was the key to getting my derailed life back on track, why did I feel so awful inside?

I flew back to Portland, and a week later got the call from the breast cancer center offering me the job. I told them I needed to think about it. And then I sat down on the couch and cried. And then I fell to my knees. And then I lay facedown on the carpet in my living room, and I wept some more.

It was the perfect job, but I was too broken to take it. I was too fragile to leave Portland. I was too devastated by what had happened on the East Coast to move back—at least for a long, long time.

I realized as I was lying there on the carpet that I had two choices. I could have the life I'd always planned—the multiple Ivy League degrees, the Manhattan apartment, the swanky job with millionaire clients, and the high-profile writing career—but I would lose my soul.

Or I could stay in Portland and work with drunk and high patients in the ER at a hospital no one had ever heard of, write essays for online magazines with small readerships, slip anonymously into church and cry with exhaustion and relief during the hymns, and continue to reconnect with God and with myself.

Making the choice about the job opportunity was agonizing, so while I considered my decision, I did what soothes me most: I took an hour-long bubble bath. I prayed the whole time that God would help me make the right choice, and give me the grace to live with the repercussions of whatever path He led me down.

The bathwater was cold when I finally decided I would turn down the job, leave Columbia, stay in Portland, and anonymously experience the restoration of my body and my soul.

I sank down, with just my nose above the water so I could breathe. And I prayed, *God, I always thought I was going to be the beautiful, fragrant rose that bloomed for You in the middle of a prominent centerpiece. But now I see that I may only ever be a crocus in the corner of Your garden.*

My tears flowed faster and faster into the bathwater, like rivers rushing toward the sea.

And I just want to tell You if that's what You have planned for me, if I am meant to be an obscure flower in the corner of the expansive garden, I will live there and I will love You and I will bloom just for You—only, always, ever.

When I came up from the water, I was clean. And I was surrendered.

CHAPTER SEVENTY-EIGHT

N O, NO, NO, NO, NO!!!" I sank down onto the edge of my bed
in disbelief, staring at my iPhone.

It was a few months after the Invisible Girls had moved to Seattle.
I had picked up my phone to call Hadhi, but her number and name
had somehow been erased from my cell phone. All of her contact
info was gone, and I had no idea how to get ahold of her.

No, please, no, I thought. I looked for the notebook where I'd
written down Amine's phone number and address but I couldn't
find it anywhere. The last time Hadhi had talked to me, she had said
something about a new apartment, so I was assuming they would've
moved by now and the address I had from Amine would be obsolete
anyway.

I felt sick to my stomach. I had lost the tenuous thread that
had kept me attached to them. I put my head in my hands, and
feeling completely at a loss for what to do next, I prayed for the
girls. I prayed for God to protect them, for God to provide for
them, and for God to somehow tell me how to get in touch with
them.

Weeks went by. I didn't tell anyone that the Invisible Girls' phone number and whereabouts had vanished from my phone, because I couldn't bear to say it out loud. Every night before I went to sleep, I prayed for Hadhi and the girls. But hours, days, weeks went by, and there was only silence. And then one evening as I was cleaning up from dinner, my phone rang. I didn't recognize the number, but I picked up anyway.

"Sahara!" a voice on the other line said.

"Fahari?" I said hesitantly, not wanting to get my hopes up.

"Yah, Sahara, yah."

"Baby, how did you get my number?"

She explained that her mom had walked down to the corner store, but left her cell phone and purse in the apartment. Fahari had riffled through the purse and found the scrap of paper I'd put in there on their last night in Portland—the one with my name and e-mail and phone number, in case they ever wanted to look me up.

"I found the number and called you," she said.

"Good girl. *Good, good girl*," I said, my voice cracking. "Where are you?" I asked.

"We moved to new apartment," Fahari said.

"Where?"

"Seattle."

"I know, but where in Seattle?" I asked.

"An apartment," she said.

"Which apartment?"

"A Seattle apartment," she said.

I groaned. How in the world was I going to figure out where they were? I asked if there were numbers on the front door, if there was a piece of mail with their new address that she could read off to me, anything. But Fahari kept saying she didn't know where they were, and didn't know how to find out.

"Do you have neighbors?" I asked.

"Yah, Sahara, yah," she said. "She's a nice lady."

"Okay, can you give the phone to your neighbor for a minute?"

As I listened on the other end, Fahari unlocked the deadbolt on the front door, walked to her neighbor's apartment, and knocked on the door. A minute later, I heard a woman's voice speaking fluent English. Fahari handed the phone to her.

"Hello?" she said skeptically.

"My name is Sarah," I said in a measured tone, wanting to convince her I wasn't crazy, wanting to ease my way into her trust without her hanging up on me. "I worked with this family in Portland— they are refugees from Somalia. They just moved to Seattle and I wanted to come visit them, but they can't tell me where they live." I paused for a minute. "Could you please tell me the name of the apartment complex where you are?"

"The Town Apartments," she said, then handed the phone back to Fahari.

"Tell that lady thank you!" I told Fahari, but it was too late. The woman had already closed and locked her door.

"Fahari, which unit are you in? Which apartment?"

"A-1," she said. "I mean, 8-1. I mean, no, I mean, wait, ash-1."

"I'm sorry, *which* apartment?"

"Ash-1," she said. "Ash-1."

"Do you mean H?"

"Sahara, do you want to talk to Lelo?" And with that, she handed the phone to the four-year-old, who told me that she cried for me every night, and asked if I could please come to Seattle and bring ten pizzas.

And then I heard Chaki yelling in the background that they wanted me to bring Justin Bieber, too. A few minutes later, while they were still passing the phone around among the five of them, we got disconnected. I tried to call back, but they didn't answer.

That weekend, I recruited my friend Stephanie to drive to Seattle with me to find them. "I know where they are," I said.

She raised her eyebrows.

"Well, I'm pretty sure."

CHAPTER SEVENTY-NINE

A FEW DAYS LATER we were in my silver Scion driving the three-hour stretch of I-5 North that connects Portland to Seattle. On the way up, I started to get nervous. What if I couldn't find them? What if they'd moved again? What if their neighbor didn't trust me, and gave me the wrong apartment complex name?

Stephanie plugged her iPod into the jack that feeds into the car's stereo. The first song came on and I said, "Not that one." She forwarded the playlist to the next song. "Not that one either," I said.

She went through about ten songs before she found one I liked. *Why am I so anxious?* I thought.

Just relax. God's in control, so you can just chill out.

When we got to the outskirts of Seattle, Stephanie took out her smart phone and googled the location of The Town Apartments. She plugged it into a map program, and we got off the freeway and started zigzagging down side streets until we got to the address. It was a set of upscale apartment buildings in a circle. The courtyard in the center of the circle featured a pool, a hot tub, and the rental office.

The sky had been cloudy for the past three hours, but as I stepped out of the car, it started to rain. Stephanie didn't have a hood on her sweater, so she stayed in the car while I went exploring.

"Where are you, apartment H-1?" I muttered as I began walking around the large circle of buildings. A, B, C, D, E, F, G…and that was it. The last building was G.

I groaned as the rain began to fall harder. I walked the circle one more time, looking to see if there were buildings I'd missed, or maybe a driveway that led to another part of the complex. But there was nothing. I went to the rental office. The lights were on, but it was locked. I knocked a few times, but no one came.

I went back to the car, opened the door, and sat in the driver's seat. This was exactly what I'd been afraid of—that somehow I had the wrong information for them, and I wasn't going to be able to find them.

Stephanie offered to help look for their building. She pulled her sweater over her head, and we split up, walking on opposite sides of the circle of buildings until we met in the center. Nothing. We knocked again on the rental office door, but no one came. The phone number was etched on the office's large glass window, so I tried calling it a few times, but just got the answering machine.

We went back to the car, got in, and sat in our seats shivering, our clothes soaked with rain. I put my head on the steering wheel and said, "Jesus, where are those girls?"

Then it occurred to me that these apartments were really nice— they probably rented for at least $1,200 per month. And I knew from helping Hadhi with her finances in the past that she probably had less than $800 per month to spend on housing.

I said, "I wonder if there's a different apartment complex that has the word *Town* in the name?"

Stephanie pulled out her phone and did a quick search. "Yes!" she said. Five miles away was another apartment complex called The Town Apartments at Riverplace. She put the address into the GPS, and in a few minutes we were there.

It was a run-down complex of marigold-colored buildings that looked like they hadn't been painted since the 1970s. The cars in the parking spaces were dented and rusting, and at least ten years old.

"This is more like it," I said. This looked like a place that would offer Section 8 housing. And the buildings were lettered from A to P. I pulled up outside the H building and got out to investigate while Stephanie sat in the running car. There was no apartment labeled H-1, so I called Hadhi's cell phone to ask which unit they were in.

Fahari answered.

"Fahari, I'm here in Seattle," I said.

"You come Seattle? Now?"

"Yes." I laughed. "I came now. I'm here."

Then I asked her if she could come outside and stand on the patio so I could find her. "Okay, Sahara," she said. "I outside now."

I kept talking to her. How was Seattle, how were her sisters, had she eaten any goat lately? We kept talking and I kept wandering around, until the voice I was hearing through the phone and through the air was the same. I found her standing on the balcony of a third-floor apartment, wearing her Somali dress and head scarf, smiling and waving at me. She led me inside, where the other girls were sitting on the floor watching TV.

When they saw me, they screamed and jumped up and ran to me, wrapping their arms around my knees and my waist, clinging to me without any sign of letting go.

"You came!" Abdallah said, her eyes brimming with tears.

"I told you I would," I said. And as I wrapped my arms around her, I remembered their last night in Portland when I cupped her scarred cheek with my hand and whispered in her ear, "No matter where you go, I promise I will always love you, and I will always find you."

CHAPTER EIGHTY

After a long group hug, I managed to untangle myself from the girls. "Where's your mom?" I asked Fahari.

"She's at the store," Fahari said.

"Which store?"

Fahari shrugged.

"Do you guys want to say hi to Stephanie?" I asked.

They nodded eagerly. I told them they should put their shoes on before we went outside, but they said they were too excited for shoes. So they ran alongside me in their bare feet, splashing through warm puddles of summer rain on the way to the car.

After they hugged Stephanie, I took the girls back inside and told Fahari to lock the door. "My friend and I are going to go get some snacks and some pizza," I said. "We'll be back in less than an hour."

While we were driving toward the pizza shop, I noticed a Dollar Tree store in a shopping plaza, and on a whim I pulled into the lot so we could pick up some art supplies for the girls. We were deciding which checkout line to stand in when a teenage girl in African robes walked in front of us. I smiled at her, wondering how big the Somali community in this town was. And then, just behind her, I saw a familiar silhouette.

"Hadhi!?" I asked.

The adult woman in flowing robes turned, and I saw that it was, in fact, Hadhi. I gave her a hug.

"What are you doing here!?" I asked her.

She laughed. "I go to store," she said.

I asked if she wanted to pick up some things for the house. "It's on me," I told her.

We took the cart back through the aisles and picked up toothpaste, deodorant, sponges, floor cleaner, Windex, laundry detergent, canned goods, cereal, and rice. After we checked out, Hadhi motioned to another woman in African robes who was standing next to the teenage girl I'd noticed earlier. "We go in your car?" she asked.

"Yes. Everyone can ride in my car."

We stacked the bags of art supplies and groceries in the back, and everyone piled in. The car was packed to the gills, but they didn't seem to mind. We dropped the other woman and her daughter off at their apartment, then stopped by the pizza shop and got two cheese pizzas and a 2-liter bottle of Coke and drove back to the apartment, where the girls were waiting eagerly for their pizza party.

While the pizzas were heating up, the girls rummaged through the bags and pulled out the stickers, coloring books, crayons, and markers we'd bought for them. Stephanie and I sat on the floor and helped them draw letters and numbers, and showed them how to color inside the lines. The girls crawled from lap to lap, hung over our shoulders, and played with our hair.

When it was time to eat, we sat in a circle and ate pizza, and then we had cookies for dessert. The girls talked about Portland, and told me they still remembered the pizza party my friends and I threw for them on the last night before they moved to Seattle.

After we cleaned up from the meal, we kept our tradition of singing the chorus of Justin Bieber's song "Baby," and then Stephanie and I said our good-byes and left.

As we were pulling out of the apartment complex, I wiped away bittersweet tears. I was so thankful we'd been able to find them and spend time with them, but I also realized how much I missed them being close by.

"Man, I love those girls," I told Stephanie.

"I know," she said.

"And I miss them *terribly*."

"I know," she said again.

And then we fell silent as the car navigated the slick Seattle side streets and merged back onto the freeway. I spent the entire three-hour drive home thinking about the Invisible Girls, wondering how to instill in them the confidence they needed to make themselves heard and valued and seen.

We drove past Reed College on the way home, and I thought of Chaki and Lelo chattering while we had driven past the school on one of our outings. I remembered the mischievous sparkle in Chaki's eyes as she informed Lelo, "We go to college."

Since then I'd often imagined how incredible it would be to send the girls to college. I made decent money working as a physician assistant, but there was no way I could pay for five college tuitions. When I realized it would take tens of thousands of dollars to accomplish this feat, I had given up the idea.

As we were driving past Reed on the way back that night, I thought of the blog I'd started about the family, and how my friends kept asking me for more stories because they couldn't get enough of these lost, soulful girls. What if there was a bigger audience? What if I wrote the Invisible Girls' story into a book, and used the proceeds to pay for their tuition?

"I know how I'm going to do it," I announced to Stephanie as we pulled into my driveway a few minutes later—the same driveway where I'd sat six months before, telling myself it was crazy to visit the home of refugees I'd met on the MAX.

"How to do what?" she asked.

"I know how I'm going to send the Invisible Girls to college," I said.

CHAPTER EIGHTY-ONE

WHEN I KNEW I was staying in Portland rather than returning to the East Coast, I decided to take the money I'd saved up for journalism school and use it as a down payment for a house instead.

After searching for a few months, I settled on a three-bedroom town house that was in my price range, and located only a few miles away from the hospital where I worked. The day after my real estate agent showed me the house, I was sitting in a mortgage broker's office waiting to find out if my application for financing had been approved.

"I got you a thirty-year mortgage at 4.75 percent interest," he said. "I could've gotten you a lower interest rate if your credit score had been a little better."

I was puzzled. I had no credit card debt, and I paid all of my bills on time. I lived below my means, and was always careful with my money. How was my credit score not perfect?

I asked to see the report, and he passed three pages across the desk. As I scanned the report, I recognized department store credit accounts that I'd opened to get a discount on purchases, but later paid off and closed out. I recognized the company that financed my student loans from undergrad. But there was a page and a half of Chase Bank loans that I had never seen before.

"These aren't mine," I said.

He raised his eyebrows. I wondered how many times he heard false claims of innocence, and if he was doubting mine now.

"I swear to God, I have no idea what these loans are for," I said. "What do I do about it?"

"You'll have to call the company," he said.

Great, I thought to myself as I left his office. *As if cancer, a breakup, and a cross-country move weren't enough, now I have to figure out who stole my identity, and how.*

The following day, after a whirlwind of signing documents, securing a mortgage, and obtaining homeowners insurance, my real estate agent called me to tell me the good news: the town house was mine.

She met me in front of my new place and handed me the keys. "Congratulations," she said. I gave her a thank-you note and a bottle of wine, and she gave me a gift card to World Market.

And then I stood there, staring at the front door, key in my hand, with the nagging feeling that something was missing. No, it was some*one*. I'd often imagined the moment when Ian and I would buy a house in San Diego, and he would scoop me up in his arms and carry me across the threshold. It never occurred to me that I might not marry Ian, or that I might buy a house by myself, and make my grand entrance alone.

My real estate agent got a call from someone, and she began explaining to them who was bringing the hot dog buns to a picnic. While she talked, she sent me an apologetic look and motioned me toward the door.

I slowly fit the key into the lock, opened the door, and stepped across the threshold. My agent waved at me and, while she continued her cell phone conversation, climbed into her car and drove away. I closed the door behind me, sat down in the empty living room with my back against the wall, and I cried.

Karina came over a few hours later, and helped me unpack my boxes. "How does it feel to own a house?" she asked.

"It feels hollow," I said as I surveyed all the empty rooms.

As I unpacked dishes and arranged them in a kitchen cabinet, I said, "Maybe I could drive downtown and ask homeless people and refugees if they want to come live with me."

"I don't think that's how it works," Karina said, laughing.

Little did I know that in a few months, God was going to literally drop a refugee family into my lap, and fill up the empty spaces in my heart with Hadhi and her five irrepressible Invisible Girls.

CHAPTER EIGHTY-TWO

A FTER MAKING THE down payment on my town house, I had a little bit of money left over. I had always wanted to see Paris, so I spent the money on a weeklong trip to France.

I woke up early the first morning I was in Europe, and couldn't get back to sleep. So I wandered around misty Paris streets until I found myself in the courtyard outside of Notre Dame Cathedral. As I stood staring up at the scrolling architecture, the bells began to ring announcing the beginning of the early-morning Mass, and I slipped into the back row to observe the service.

As I sat there listening to a priest deliver the homily in French, I noticed the cross at the front of the cathedral. Unlike other crucifixes, Jesus wasn't hanging on this cross. Instead, His lifeless body was lying in the arms of Mary, who was kneeling at the foot of the cross, weeping over her crucified son.

I'd always aspired to be like Mary. I wanted to be a special girl who caught God's eye and became an instrument to share His love with the world. The Mary I'd learned about in Sunday school was the virgin who received the good news from the angel, who knelt by the manger watching Emmanuel take His first breaths. But the statue of

Mary kneeling heartbroken at the foot of the cross reminded me that her life was not always so enviable.

For the rest of her life, people who didn't believe in the Immaculate Conception accused her of lying about her relationship with Joseph or, worse, of selling herself to Roman soldiers. She listened to people call her Son a charlatan and a lunatic. And finally, she watched as her Son was killed by the ones He'd come to rescue. Mary was the conduit through which God poured His love for the world, but that love cost her everything. And as she watched the world reject her Son, it broke her heart.

The flight home from Paris was ten hours long, which gave me a lot of time to think. As the plane passed over the Atlantic Ocean, then over New York City, and then on toward my home in Portland, I realized how much energy I had spent that year trying to go back. Back to the girl I was before cancer, back to the body I had before all the scars, back to my life on the East Coast. But now, as I absorbed the enormity of the expanse that separated East Coast from West, I saw that I could never go back; I could only ever go forward from here. My old life was gone, leaving me with no other option but to live the new, messy-but-precious life that was waiting for me in Portland.

Over the past few years, I had spent most of my savings on cancer treatments that kept me from dying, and most of my energy on emotional and spiritual growth that kept me from *wanting* to die. During the first year after my cancer diagnosis, I had prayed every night for God to take me Home to be with Him if life wasn't going to get any better, and I felt as if my prayer had gone unnoticed or unanswered because I had to keep praying it. Now it dawned on me that I had received His response because, morning after morning, I kept waking up.

As the wheels of the plane touched down on the runway of Portland International Airport—the airport where I'd landed two years before as a bald, broken girl after barely escaping death—I thought of the Shakespeare line: "We owe God a death."

Between the cancer and the pneumonia, I should have died by now. But God had mercifully healed me. So for now, until He cashed out my chips, what I owed Him was not a death, but a well-lived life.

Part of my plan to enjoy life in Portland included doing interesting things just because, just for me. Shortly after I returned from Paris, I signed up for French lessons because I'd always wanted to learn the language.

I was riding the MAX downtown for my first lesson when a little Somali girl started playing peekaboo with me.

As Chaki slept in my arms and Lelo giggled over her "game" that first day, I started thinking of Mary again. Not just the Madonna with the infant Christ child, but also the mother weeping for her crucified Son. I recognized that same paradox in myself as the train traveled the tracks that were dappled in warm fall sunshine.

In spite of all the dangers and toils and snares I'd just endured, my wounded heart was already beating with affection and compassion for these beautiful girls. And that's when I realized:

Love will cost you dearly.
And it will break your heart.
But in the end, it will save the world.

EPILOGUE

A WEEK AFTER the Invisible Girls moved away, I met Kristin, one of the other Big Sisters, for dinner on a Saturday evening. We were going to eat at a Cajun restaurant and then catch a movie at the second-run theater across the street.

Over bowls of spicy jambalaya and plates of crumbly cornbread, we talked about the Invisible Girls and how sad we were that they'd gone. We reminisced about the unusual way God had brought the girls into our lives, and all of the amazing things that had happened over the past few months.

Kristin said the Somali family reminded her of the Bible story of Hagar, the pregnant girl who was fleeing into the desert when God found her and told her what to do next.

"Did you know Hagar was the only person in the Bible to name God?" Kristin asked.

I shook my head.

"She called him *El Roi*, which means *the God who sees.*"

I remembered seeing the girls for the first time on the train—not just laying eyes on them, but really seeing them. I recognized them because I, too, had been a girl in a fundamentalist culture and had struggled to emerge from yards of fabric and years of hiding. I, too, had been a refugee of sorts, fleeing a life-threatening experience and ending up in Portland with nothing but clothes.

So when I saw the Invisible Girls on the train, I immediately knew them. Because I'd been an Invisible Girl, too.

As we were putting our coats on, we wondered aloud if something this incredible would ever happen to us again. I told Kristin I felt the way I often feel after I write an article that gets published to positive reviews—worried that it was a once-in-a-lifetime accomplishment, worried that the muse will never come again.

As we were walking across the street, I noticed a circle of scantily clad women who were smoking outside a dive bar. Just as we were walking by them, they all started yelling at one young woman in the circle, telling her to leave and go home because they didn't want to have anything to do with her.

Kristin and I kept walking. We passed a Chinese restaurant, and Kristin said she wondered what their food was like.

A quiet voice behind us said, "I heard it's not very good."

We walked to the corner and were waiting to cross the street. Out of the corner of my eye, I saw the young woman who had been walking behind us lean against the window of a closed Starbucks. She held an unlit cigarette between her teeth while she searched through the pockets of her black leather jacket and black skinny jeans for a lighter.

As I was observing the girl, Kristin said, "I think she was talking to us. When she said, 'I heard it's not very good,' she was answering my question about the restaurant."

Kristin and I looked at each other, then back at the girl.

"We have to talk to her," I said.

We abandoned our plans for the movie and approached the girl.

I didn't know what to say to her, or how to talk to her without freaking her out. I said, "My friend and I are hanging out together tonight, and we were wondering if you'd like to join us."

Her eyes lit up, and she nodded eagerly. She told us that her favorite pub was just a block away, and we agreed to follow her there. As we walked across the street, I noticed her strappy black stiletto heels, tight jeans, and low-cut tank top. Her hair was disheveled and dyed bleach-blond, with random chunks cut to various lengths.

When she pulled a roll of hundred-dollar bills out of her pocket to pay for her three-dollar whiskey, I surmised how she made a living. Kristin and I each ordered a drink, too, and then we sat down at a table and began to talk with her.

She told us her name was Carla, and she'd recently moved to Portland from Las Vegas. She said her first memory of Portland was watching it snow. Before she'd moved here, she'd always seen piles of snow, but during her first week in Portland, she had actually seen snow fall. It was the first time she realized that the piles she'd seen before were comprised of unique, individual flakes.

Then, without any prompting, she began to tell us about her life. The abusive boyfriend she'd escaped who had held her down on the floor and spit in her face as he raped her. Her friends who were in similarly abusive relationships. Her distance from her family. The nights she spent lying in bed, staring into the darkness, calling out to God. And her conclusion that because her life continued to be unspeakably hard, He did not exist, or at least was not listening to her.

She stopped talking and eyed us suspiciously. "Why aren't you drinking?" she asked. We each took an obligatory sip of our drinks.

"Why are you even talking to me?" she asked.

At first I tried to say something light because I was worried I'd scare her off. "You looked like a cool person to hang out with," I said with a casual shrug.

But she didn't buy it. She kept asking why we'd talked to her, why we'd asked to hang out with her. Finally, I leaned closer, put my hand on her arm, and said, "Because, Carla, God wants you to know that He didn't create you to live in a random pile of dirty snow. God made you like a snowflake—individual, unique, precious."

She began to cry, tears splashing into her empty glass. I took her hand and held it while she wept. A few minutes later, she became anxious, stood up and grabbed her jacket, and said she had to go. She was almost out the door when I called to her.

"Carla," I said.

She turned around.

"Remember, when you're calling out to God at night, He hears you. And when you feel invisible, like a flake lost in a pile of dirty snow, He sees you."

"He sees me?" she asked.

I nodded.

Her eyes lit up, and then she turned to leave. As I watched her disappear into the night, it suddenly occurred to me that Invisible Girls are everywhere.

Do you see them?

POSTSCRIPT

One of my biggest motivations for writing this book was so I could use the proceeds to start a college fund for the girls. Getting an education was crucial in my own journey of going from an invisible girl to a strong, independent woman, and I wanted to give these girls the same opportunity. Plus, it seemed the least I could do for my little Somali sisters who had given me their priceless affection and friendship when I was at the lowest point of my life.

After I'd shopped the proposal around to several publishers, Jericho Books made me an offer. I was elated.

The day after I signed the book deal for *The Invisible Girls*, I raced up to Seattle to throw the girls a party. Since they'd moved to Seattle, I'd driven up every two months to check on them and take them pizza, but this time I wanted our visit to be special.

On the way, I bought five backpacks and filled them with notebooks, pencils, crayons, and mittens. Then I stopped at a grocery store and picked up pizza, oranges, ice cream sandwiches, and Sunny D, as well as pink paper plates and napkins.

When I got to their apartment, I knocked on the door. I heard Chaki's voice on the other side asking, "Who is it?" in Somali.

"Baby, it's me," I said.

She flung the door open and jumped up into my arms. Then she turned her head to yell into the apartment, "It's Sahara! It's Sahara!"

The four other girls came running outside, clamoring to see who could hug me first. Fahari noticed the grocery bags, and leaned up to whisper in my ear.

"That's food for us?"

"Yes!" I said. "Who wants to have a party?"

The girls squealed as they picked up the grocery bags and carried the food inside. Lelo noticed a large garbage bag I'd brought with me that contained the five backpacks.

"Can I take for you that one?" she asked.

"No, that's okay," I said. "That's a surprise for later."

"A surprise? For *me*?" She was an inch taller than when I'd seen her last, but her large brown eyes still had the same sparkle.

I scooped her up and she started giggling.

"Yes, baby," I said. "The surprise is for you. It's for all of you."

Carrying Lelo in one arm and the garbage bag in the other, I walked into the apartment, where Hadhi was waiting to greet me with a hug. She had already turned on the oven to bake the pizza, and was pouring juice into a single large cup for all of us to share. The girls were laying out the pink plates and napkins on the empty dining room floor.

Half an hour later, as we sat in a circle eating a feast of their favorite foods, I announced, "I wrote a book about us!"

They stopped eating their pizza and oranges as I continued, "And people who love you are going to buy the story and read it, and we're going to use the money to send you to college."

They began squealing and jumping around, giddy at the thought of going to college in America. I looked at Hadhi while her girls were dancing around the room.

"It's okay if they go to college?" I asked her.

"Yah, Sarah, yah," she said as she took my hand in hers. "America very good. College very good."

When their excitement had died down, the girls came back to the circle. I handed each of them an ice cream sandwich and a backpack filled with school supplies. As they were unpacking the surprises, I asked each of them what they wanted to be when they grew up.

I had asked them this question when they were younger, and each girl told me she wanted to be a ballerina or Barbie or a princess. At one point, Chaki had told me she wanted to be a puddle.

But the girls had grown up since then, and now their answers were more grounded. Fahari spoke up first. She'd gotten a little taller and curvier since I'd seen her last, but she was still timid.

"I want to be a wife and a mom," she said, blushing. Hadhi smiled at her daughter's answer.

Sadaka went next. As she eyed me with a mischievous grin, she said, "I'm going to be a doctor. Because I like the doctor who takes care of me."

I asked Chaki what she wanted to be when she grew up, but she had already put on her backpack and was too busy skipping around the room to answer.

When it was Lelo's turn, she looked up at me and squinted. "Girls—they can be bus drivers or no?" Her English was still awkward, but improving.

"Yes, baby," I said. "Girls can be anything they want to be."

With an emphatic nod she said, "Then I to drive a school bus for kids."

Abdallah was sitting closest to me, and she went last. Like her sisters, she was getting taller, but she was still thin with a small circular scar on her cheek. When I asked her what she wanted to be when she grew up, she looked down at the floor.

"What is it?" I asked.

"You promise you won't laugh?" she asked her sisters. They giggled at her question, then nodded in agreement.

"Do you promise, Sahara?" she asked me.

"I promise," I said as I wrapped my arms around her and kissed the top of her head.

She looked up at me, and with tears brimming in her eyes she said softly, "Sahara, when I grow up...I want to be just like you."

All of the proceeds from this book are going toward the girls' college fund. If you'd like to contribute, please mail a donation to:

Invisible Girls Trust Fund
c/o Ameriprise Financial Services, Inc.
1400 NW Irving Street, Suite 324
Portland, OR 97209

To book Sarah as a speaker, contact www.ChaffeeManagement.com or call (615) 300-9699.

ACKNOWLEDGMENTS

Thank you Wendy, for taking a chance on me.

Thank you Greg and Jim, for being my advocates.

Thank you Chelsea, Harry, Jake, Sarah, Andrea, and Shanon, for working so hard to make this happen.

Thank you Adrienne, for helping me turn a story into an honest-to-goodness book.

Thank you Karrie and Betsy, for putting up with me, even when I was in writing mode.

Thank you Simons & Fox, for finding the writer in me.

Thank you Stephanie, for making me laugh.

Thank you Alex, for helping me hope.

Thank you Karina, for being one of the few constants in my life.

Thank you Karen, for insisting that I had a book in me.

Thank you Michelle, Dr. DiGiovanni, Dr. Fusi, Dr. Zuckerman, and Dr. Smith, for saving my life.

Thank you Randy and Nanci, for showing me how to change the world with a pen.

Thank you Kristin S., for walking through the valley of shadows with me.

Thank you Kristin G., for reminding me about the God Who Sees.

Thank you Doug, for walking in when everyone else was walking out.

Thanks to my Imago Dei community, for giving me a safe place to
heal.

Thanks to my family, for celebrating with me at my best, and loving
me at my worst.

Most importantly, thanks to my precious God and Savior, for never
letting go.

ABOUT THE AUTHOR

SARAH THEBARGE is a speaker and author who grew up as a pastor's kid in Lancaster, Pennsylvania. She earned a master's degree in medical science from Yale School of Medicine and was studying journalism at Columbia University when she was diagnosed with breast cancer at age twenty-seven. Sarah's writing has appeared in *Christianity Today*, BurnsideWriters.com, *Relevant*, TheOoze.com, *Raysd*, and *Just Between Us*. Her writing for *Christianity Today's This Is Our City* project won first prize from the National Evangelical Press Association. She currently lives in Santa Barbara, California.

READING GROUP GUIDE

Go deeper into the story of *The Invisible Girls* with our new Reading Group Guide. The four sections contain questions derived from chapters 1–20, 21–40, 41–60, and 61–Epilogue, respectively. We hope you will use this guide to gain thoughtful insights into the author's journey of self-discovery in *The Invisible Girls*—and perhaps to learn something new about yourself along the way.

QUESTIONS FOR DISCUSSION

Section One—Chapters 1-20

1. Sarah Thebarge begins *The Invisible Girls* with the Ralph Waldo Emerson quote: "I am invisible, understand, simply because people refuse to see me." What did this quote mean to you before you started reading? After finishing the first section of this book, what does that quote say to you now?

2. In Chapters 2 and 3, Sarah details some of the emotional and physical horrors she endured as a young woman diagnosed with breast cancer. In addition to fighting for her life, the author suffered the agony of learning she would never bear children. How does the seemingly ordinary scene at Karina's house in Chapter 3 underscore the enormity of Sarah's losses?

3. Sarah seems to have a love-hate relationship with her strict, fundamentalist upbringing, which included outdated fashions, a ban on movies and makeup, and the expectation that women will be content as housewives and mothers. How did this worldview affect her physically and emotionally? How did it shape her character?

4. Sarah describes herself as a "pastor's kid" and details some of the childhood games she and her siblings played and the messages they received. How does Sarah use these stories to show us her growing confusion and determination to be different? How does she want to be different from the women in her culture?

5. After Sarah visits the Somali family's apartment for the first time, she goes home and calls a friend who works for an international relief agency. Sarah admits that her knowledge of Africa is "embarrassingly scant." She realizes that neither her religious upbringing nor her Ivy League degrees taught her much about the atrocities taking place in many countries around the world. What do you think our education should include? How can we develop a more global worldview?

6. As Sarah begins to visit the Somali family, she realizes how many cultural differences stand between them. After Chaki poops on the floor in Chapter 14, she states, "It seems to me that anytime you encounter another culture, there is bound to be surprise, fascination, disorientation—sometimes even disgust and offense." How did you feel when you visited or interacted with people from other cultures than your own? Were you uncomfortable? What did you learn from the experience?

7. After Sarah's sister Hannah almost died, Sarah's parents told God they would no longer try to possess or control their children. So when Sarah decides to go to college in California, they don't stand in her way. How does her choice to leave home change her? Does it free her? What choices did you make as a young adult that freed or imprisoned you?

8. When Sarah meets Ian, a whole new world is opened to her—one filled with love and money. She experiences filet mignon and beach houses, as well as romance and the prospect of marriage. How does the final sentence in Chapter 18 foreshadow the end of this fairy tale?

9. Sarah questions her relationship with the Somali family and wonders if they are becoming codependent, if she is helping or hurting both them and herself. How can acts of charity and

compassion become messy and draining? How have you found ways to give without encouraging dependence, or enabling addictions or poor life choices?

10. At the end of Chapter 20, Sarah takes us back to her cancer diagnosis and how she begged God not to leave her as she sobbed in Ian's arms. When the girls snuggle up to Sarah at the end of Chapter 19, she sings "Amazing Grace." Do you think she chose this song purposely or subconsciously? How is this a telling moment in Sarah's healing process? What do you think it reveals about her faith after her cancer journey?

Section Two—Chapters 21–40

1. Sarah describes breast cancer as not only terrifying and painful, but also embarrassing. She tells us she feels "vulnerable to and violated by this disease that made my hidden parts everyone's primary concern." How did this description make you feel? Can you relate to Sarah's embarrassment?

2. What does Sarah do so she can remember what her breasts look like? Why does the impending loss of her breasts feel so devastating? How do breasts represent femininity?

3. The night before her mastectomy, Sarah prays for God to take away her cancer. She believes He can do it, but He doesn't. Sarah decides that God sentenced her to have cancer on purpose. Do you agree? Why or why not? What have you encountered in life that shook your faith to the core? How did you work through it?

4. While singing "Amazing Grace" to the Somali girls, Sarah recalls her long, painful recovery from her mastectomy. Then she

thinks of the suffering the Somali family has endured. How does this comparison and her love for Chaki help her understand the way Jesus sees us as His children?

5. After her surgery, Sarah feels alone and abandoned. Her church friends don't drop off their promised meals or visit her, and Ian begins to pull away. How can isolation be as dangerous to our souls as cancer is to our bodies?

6. Why do you think friends disappeared after Sarah's surgery? How do tragic events sometimes make people uncomfortable? Do you think Sarah's friends didn't care, or do you think they just didn't know what to say or do?

7. In Chapter 32, Sarah's friend Stephan commits a small act of kindness that lets her know he remembers her. What does he tell her, and why can't she believe it?

8. During a Christmas Eve service, Sarah remembers that *In excelsis Deo* is Latin for "God in the highest" and she thinks that she doesn't want God to be in the highest—she wants Him to be with her at her lowest. People often say that if we feel distant from God, it's because we have drifted. He remains steady all the time. How does cancer make Sarah feel about this sentiment? Do you agree?

9. At her birthday dinner, Sarah tells God she can hang on as long as life doesn't get any worse. Just following this prayer, her hair catches on fire as she blows out the candles on her birthday cake. Do you think this was God's answer? Why or why not?

10. How does Hadhi's selfless parenting reassure Sarah of God's love?

Section Three—Chapters 41–60

1. As soon as we experience Sarah feeling some peace in the present in Chapter 40, we watch as she is plunged back into despair in the past in Chapter 41. Her cancer recurs, and her cohort in cancer, Libby, dies. How did these highs and lows so close together keep you engaged in the story?

2. Sarah's Thanksgiving with the Invisible Girls changed her perception of the holiday and its meaning. What does Thanksgiving mean to you? What do you have to be thankful for? How do you celebrate in the midst of sorrow?

3. By Chapter 47, Sarah has lost her health, breasts, hair, fiancé, ability to have children, friends, work, school, disability claim, and car. Then her cancer recurs again. In the face of such enormous losses, how does one keep having faith in God?

4. Sarah has conflicting views of God. How did she view Him as a child, and how was she learning to see Him before cancer? As a child, how did you picture God? How do you see Him now?

5. Hadhi proclaims that "America is broken." What image of America did she have before arriving, and how has she become disillusioned?

6. How did the riddle "How do you eat an elephant?" help Sarah when she felt overwhelmed? What do you do when you don't feel like your efforts will ever be enough?

7. What does Sarah realize about Hadhi at the end of Chapter 58? How does it make her look at Hadhi differently?

8. Every time Sarah is desperate or close to death, something occurs that offers a tiny bit of hope. When Rajah appears at the ER, does his reading of Psalm 23 feel like hope or a eulogy? Why is this scene significant to Sarah's story?

Section Four—Chapters 61–Epilogue

1. Sarah remembers that in *The Message* version of the Bible, Romans 10:13 says: "Everyone who says, 'Help, God!' gets help." How does this verse give her the courage to begin fighting to live?

2. Human beings are created with a fight-or-flight instinct that kicks in when we are in danger. When Sarah decides to move to Portland for a fresh start, do you think she is fighting or fleeing? How do you react when tragedy strikes or life feels overwhelming?

3. When Sarah discovers that the Invisible Girls are moving to Seattle, how does she react? While Sarah was meeting the family's physical needs, what were they giving back to her? Which is more valuable: hope or healing?

4. How does Sarah's view of God change when she begins to see Him as "my Father and the Great Physician"? How can pain be a good thing in our lives?

5. In Chapter 77, why does Sarah say that having the life she'd always planned would cost her soul? What do you do when you have a bad feeling about something that looks like a good opportunity?

6. What does Sarah's bubble bath represent spiritually? What happens to her when she finally gives up her own dreams, her own ideals?

7. Sarah tells the Invisible Girls, "No matter where you go, I promise I will always love you, and I will always find you." How does this promise echo Sarah's spiritual journey?

8. When Sarah announces that she will pay for the Invisible Girls to go to college by writing a book about them and using the

proceeds to pay for their tuition, how did you feel when you realized you were holding a copy of that book?

9. Among the themes of loss, hope, faith, and surrender that run throughout *The Invisible Girls*, there is also the theme of acceptance. Accepting that we don't always see the whole picture. Accepting that something can be gained from loss. How is acceptance different from resignation?

10. How did this book affect you? Do you think it helps answer the question "Why does God allow bad things to happen to good people?" How do you think Sarah would answer that question now?

Thanks for reading and discussing *The Invisible Girls*. To learn more about Sarah and the Invisible Girls, visit www.SarahThebarge.com.